Lost and Found II

LOST AND FOUND II

*More Historic and Natural Landmarks
Under Southern California Skies*

BY ELIZABETH POMEROY

**MANY
MOONS**
PRESS

Lost and Found II: More Historic and Natural Landmarks Under Southern California Skies, First Edition, was produced by Regina Books and printed by Cushing-Malloy, Inc..

Book design is by Mark Morrall Dodge.

The watercolor paintings on the cover are by Joseph Stoddard. The front shows Eaton Canyon, Pasadena; the back, Arroyo Seco, Pasadena. He also provided the pen and ink sketches done on location for the section divider pages.

Cover design and art direction are by Hortensia Chu. She also created the Many Moons Press logo.

ISBN 0-9700481-2-2

MANY MOONS PRESS

P.O. Box 94505
Pasadena, California 91109

Contents

SOUTH

EAST

Preface

Like our first volume of *Lost and Found,* this is a book of stories and also a guide to historic places. The emphasis here will lead you to some outdoor discoveries: parks, nature centers, and gardens, under Southern California skies.

These articles originally appeared in my series of newspaper columns called "Lost and Found," which has run for seven years in the *San Gabriel Valley Tribune,* the *Pasadena Star-News,* and the *Whittier Daily News.* I am grateful to Cathie Lou Parker, who first gave me the opportunity to write the column.

The area covered by this book is the San Gabriel Valley and nearby. The four sections, North, South, East, and West, should make it easier for you to plan outings as you explore beyond your own city.

I like to use my Thomas Guide (or regional map) as a kind of urban geography text. There I see the topography of hills and streams underlying our towns, and the broad sweep of valleys and lands where little settlements once grew up. At a closer level, place names attract our curiosity, and so do the patches of green indicating parks or natural areas. My eye goes straight to those bits of green, as open spaces for family fun which may also have a rich history.

Just a few suggestions for your history-hunting with this book: call a site before you visit, especially if you will be traveling a distance. The open hours sometimes change with the seasons, and you may find that a special event is coming up. Also, allow the time for a walk in the area you've chosen. You'll see more and discover no end of things to jot in your notes (restaurants, shops, or that perfect grove for a picnic).

Your camera or sketch pad can be a worthy companion, capturing a memory or sharpening your eye. "Seeking comes before seeing."

There are many ways to help sustain the historic gems you will find in this book. You could leave a contribution, or buy a memento. Many of these sites offer special books or other publications not found in regular bookstores. Your local history shelf can thrive with unusual additions, as you explore. The gift of your time is precious too, and volunteering will put you in the heart of history.

Besides showing you these lost and found gems, I would like to give you ideas of how to continue this hunting, in your own directions. I researched these topics in history archives of the towns, public libraries, local historical societies, even chambers of commerce. Historic markers may open long but rewarding quests. Curators or volunteers at one historic site will suggest others. They welcome your questions, and you can follow the threads of historical connections for as long as you enjoy the hunt.

There are many other lost and found treasures, and more become available all the time, as vintage buildings are rescued or open spaces set aside for public use. They all have stories for you to find.

Many thanks to Richard Burns and Mark Dodge, "the producers" in the making of this book. Hortensia Chu has truly been a presiding spirit, designing the cover and overseeing the project with her artist's eye. Once again Joseph Stoddard has provided his elegant watercolors for the front and back covers, and four original drawings to grace the inner geography of the book. Thank you one and all.

I am grateful also to the curators, archivists, and park officials who helped me track down these true tales of history. And to my readers, friends and encouraging family, warm thanks for joining me on these outings, and may we have many more journeys together.

Elizabeth Pomeroy
Pasadena, California
July 2002

Green Hotel, Pasadena

Christmas Tree Lane

✧ *Altadena* ✧

A ROUTE OF MEDITATION, a speedway for the earliest automobiles, a focus of civic pride: Altadena's Christmas Tree Lane has been all these and more. The history of this botanical landmark, now on the National Register of Historic Places, is a human history too.

135 beautiful deodar cedar trees line a mile of Santa Rosa Avenue, from Woodbury Road to Altadena Drive, ascending a steady grade. The deodars are evergreen, reaching 80 feet tall with a potential spread of 40 feet. Natives of the Himalayas, they grow to a pyramidal form, with the uppermost top bending as though nodding, while the lowest branches may brush the ground.

The Altadena deodars were planted on the 900-acre property of brothers Fred and John Woodbury. They had come from Iowa and acquired the northern part of Rancho San Pasqual. Fred laid out Santa Rosa Avenue in 1882. Several years later his brother, impressed by

beautiful deodars he saw in Italy, sent seeds to Fred who raised little trees and set them out along the avenue, where they flourished.

Meanwhile, the dirt straightaway proved tempting for hill-climbing contests of early motorists. A chain-driven Dusenberg was a big hit there in 1909. Residents along the road later shared the care of the trees, even washing them off after dusty summers.

In 1920 the trees were first lighted for the Christmas holidays. Fred Nash, a Pasadena merchant and Altadena resident, had the idea. The Pasadena Kiwanis Club sponsored the program, and the Southern California Edison Co. donated the power for many years.

The lighting ceremonies each year became a town "open house", with firemen's band and community singing. In 1923, the Citizens Association invited 90 towns and villages within a radius of 70 miles to join the festivity. The Pacific Electric Railway put on extra streetcars for the season, and the American Legion brought convalescing World War I soldiers from the La Vina sanitarium in the foothills.

In the 1930s some 55,000 cars drove the tree-lined mile each Christmastime. Newspapers in 1937 reported that a "first-hand word picture" would be broadcast nationwide on fledgling NBC radio, with the King and Queen of the Deodars describing the sight as they slowly rode down the avenue.

The deodars have been lighted every year since 1920 except for the War Years of 1941-45 and the energy crisis of 1973. The drive among hundreds of twinkly lights took on a meditative tone. Said Fred Nash, "we would never allow anything to detract from the silent beauty of the trees and the inspiration they radiate." Another visitor agreed: "We have made a deliberate approach to our Deodars—haste does not belong with trees. Then we began our pilgrimage of a mile up this famed Avenue."

Today 115 of the original trees and 20 newer ones form a canopy of deepest green. The trees are lighted from mid-December to New Year's day and are inspiring in any season.

How to get there: From the 210 Freeway, exit at Lake Ave., and drive north; turn left on Woodbury Rd. to Santa Rosa Ave. Turn right and you are on Christmas Tree Lane.

Mount Lowe Park

✧ *Altadena* ✧

IT'S JUST A NARROW GREEN CRESCENT, long enough for a good uphill jog or a round of frisbie with your dog. But how did it get here, this curvy little park running up the center of Mount Lowe Drive in Altadena?

This is a genuine relic from Southern California's famed Mount Lowe Railway. It was the right-of-way for the electric trolleys of the Pasadena and Mount Wilson Railway, as they approached Rubio Canyon and the mountains beyond. The railway carried thousands of visitors aloft from 1893 to 1937.

This marvel of mountain engineering is almost completely gone now, but finding its traces in the San Gabriel Mountains and also in Pasadena and Altadena is a wonderful treasure hunt.

You could begin with a book, say "Mount Lowe: the Railway in the Clouds," by Charles Seims. Or consult the exhibits and maps at the Pasadena Museum of History, on the corner of Walnut Street

and Orange Grove Boulevard in Pasadena. The Altadena Historical Society has great resources on the railway too.

The railway was the dream of Thaddeus Lowe, an inventor and Civil War balloonist, and David MacPherson, a brilliant civil engineer. From Rubio Canyon their cable cars lifted travelers up the "Great Incline", the steep slope of Echo Mountain. The Incline track was laid at an average grade of 59% and rose 1,500 vertical feet, with ascending and descending cars counter-balancing each other. Opening Day for the Incline was July 4, 1893.

Above, Lowe built the four-story Echo Mountain House, a comfortable hotel of 70 rooms, with nearby observatory, powerhouse and a small zoo.

Later the Alpine Division of the railway swung deeper into the mountains, chiseling its way through granite or soaring into midair on curving trestles. Its destination was the Alpine Tavern, a Swiss-style hotel with dining room, music room, circulating library and a big mountain fireplace. The railway drew visitors from all over the country. The trains climbed 3,100 feet in just under six miles, sometimes taking guests from the sunny valley up into snow.

It was a bold investment and Lowe dreamed of extending his line even higher. But fire destroyed the Echo Mountain House in 1900 and then Lowe lost his venture. Henry Huntington bought the railway in 1901 and ran his Red Cars (the Pacific Electric line) to Rubio Canyon. He continued the popular service, expanding the Alpine Tavern with several bungalows.

But eventually the Depression and natural forces struck the famed railway a double punch. Fire gutted the Alpine Tavern in 1936. The Railway made its last run in December 1937. In March of 1938, colossal rains wrecked most of the remaining track.

The U.S. Forest Service has removed all but the foundations of the hotels. But you can hike to these, and along historic right-of-way that still has railroad ties showing. Consult any hiking guide to our mountains for these adventures.

How to get there: To reach Mount Lowe Park, exit the 210 Freeway at Lake Ave. and drive north. Turn right on Dolores Dr., left on Mount Curve Ave. and right on Mount Lowe Dr. Call the Pasadena Museum of History at (626) 577-1660.

Mountain View Cemetery

✧ Altadena ✧

HAVE YOU EVER VISITED the oldest cemetery in your town?
You will find there a mixture of history, art, and forest—probably
some of the town's oldest and most interesting trees.

Residents of Pasadena and Altadena share this heritage at Mountain
View Cemetery in Altadena, established by Pasadena's founders in
1882. The new village of Pasadena had been neatly divided for fruit
groves just eight years before, in 1874, by settlers from Indiana.

As members of the new colony died, they were laid to rest at
cemeteries in Los Angeles or San Gabriel (the pioneer cemetery now
beside the Church of our Saviour.) Some burials were in the family
lands along Pasadena's Arroyo Seco or in the mountains.

When Colonel Jabez Banbury decided to sell some of his property,
which is currently the Wrigley Estate on Pasadena's Orange Grove
Boulevard, the family graves there raised a dilemma. So fellow
pioneer Levi Giddings offered land he owned farther north to become

the colony's first cemetery. The earlier remains were moved there and by the end of 1883, Mountain View Cemetery had 24 burials.

In the 1890s, Pasadena held Memorial Day parades with bands and bicycles, Union and Confederate veterans together, marching up Fair Oaks Boulevard to this cemetery. Photographs in the Pasadena Historical Museum show families picnicking, with flags and flowers placed among the grave markers.

Today, you can stop in the office for a Mini-Historical Tour booklet and map of the grounds. Then set off on a walk, in search of history, art, and the trees.

Notice the memorial sculpture. Children's graves are marked with tiny lambs; other themes include deftly carved draperies, lilies, and logs, sometimes with rustic "twig" lettering. The obelisks were fashionable after the Washington Monument was completed in 1884. Victorian grave mottoes were often simple, such as "Gone Home" or "At Rest."

History abounds here, and the booklet will guide you to many familiar names. The large family of Thaddeus Lowe is here. He was the Civil War balloonist and entrepreneur of the Mount Lowe Railway. The grave of Henry H. Markham, Governor of California in the 1890s, is nearby. Beside the Founders' Circle is the Giddings family plot, all relatives of Joshua Reed Giddings, the anti-slavery statesman from Ohio who fostered the "underground railroad."

Charles Richter, developer of the Richter scale for measuring earthquakes, is resting here. Much of Mt. Wilson history is represented too, including the graves of George Ellery Hale, astronomer and first director of the Mt. Wilson Solar Observatory, also W.K. Henninger who homesteaded at Henninger Flats on the slopes of the mountain, and others.

Sycamores, eucalyptus and oaks dot the sunny expanse of Mountain View Cemetery. What names and memories can you find in your own town's pioneer cemetery?

How to get there: Mountain View is at 2400 N. Fair Oaks Ave. From the 210 Freeway, exit at Fair Oaks and drive north. Call (626) 794-7133.

Arcadia Historical Museum
✧ *Arcadia* ✧

SOMETIMES A MUSEUM of a city's history can give you good ideas for organizing your own family's history. The Arcadia Historical Museum has a practical method for its displays: a simple time line.

This new museum was opened in 2001 and is still being discovered by history buffs. It presents material gathered since the founding of the Arcadia Historical Society in 1954. These objects had been shown earlier in a temporary building. Bringing order to a wealth of collectibles, the museum has arranged them in the time line.

Historical periods follow each other as the visitor walks along the displays. The earliest is the Native American period, with artifacts from the Gabrieleno Indians, so named by padres at the San Gabriel Mission. Then the time of Mexican rule with California's last Mexican governor, Pio Pico, who granted the lands of present-day Arcadia to the Scottish trader Hugo Reid in 1845.

Reid's 13,000 acre property, called Rancho Santa Anita, covered much of the western San Gabriel Valley, from the mission north to the San Gabriel Mountains. This vast spread was finally acquired by E. J. "Lucky" Baldwin in 1875.

Baldwin had made his fortune in the silver mines of the Comstock lode. He soon purchased 46,000 more acres for his Rancho Santa Anita, and developed famous horse racing stables, vineyards, and orchards with thousands of fruit trees. Later subdividing his land, he announced it was the climate he was selling.

Arcadia was incorporated as an 11-square mile city in 1903, with Baldwin as mayor. By then it was a community of small farms, with a vibrant chicken industry. The chicken period passed into the present residential city. Other steps along this historical way were the heyday of Baldwin's Santa Anita Racetrack, and later the restoration of his estate as the Los Angeles County Arboretum.

So runs the Museum's time line, across two and a half centuries of events. The exhibits show us items of daily life all along the way. They are unusually clear and visible: the stone tools used by the Native Americans, the ledger of a farm business, the sign used by a housewife telling the iceman how much ice to leave at her kitchen door.

And how does this relate to your own family history? As you gather for the holidays, or at your family reunion next summer, you might create your own family time line. Have everyone bring an object or two from earlier generations—your grandfather's watch, and the pieced quilt carefully kept for years—and arrange these in a time line. The eldest members present can fill in the stories. Gather family photos too and place them in your time line. There is much to learn, and you'll honor your family by organizing its treasures.

How to get there: For more ideas on enjoying history visit the Ruth and Charles Gilb Arcadia Historical Museum at 380 W. Huntington Dr. From the 210 Freeway, exit at Baldwin Ave. and drive south; turn left on Huntington. Call (626) 446-8512.

Hugo Reid Adobe
✧ *Arcadia* ✧

HAVE YOU STARTED your file on Southern California adobes yet? As you gather articles, you'll see the variety of these little earthen buildings. You'll learn too how their histories crisscross, with the same people and ranchos reappearing in an early California tapestry.

Consider the Hugo Reid Adobe, on the grounds of the Los Angeles County Arboretum in Arcadia. The house was built about 1839 for Scottish-born Hugo Reid, who traded in South America, then became a citizen of Mexican California. He received provisional title to the Rancho Santa Anita, 13,319 acres, and showed his intent to settle by building an adobe house.

The bricks were of sun-dried clay mixed with straw. The flat roof was daubed with tar ("brea") from pits in Los Angeles, then covered with dried cane. Here Reid entertained many visitors with his Gabrielino Indian wife Victoria and her four children, whom he had adopted.

To strengthen his claim, Reid planted wheat, 10,000 grapevines and about 1,000 fruit trees. Soon his cattle were producing well in the trade of tallow and hides, the latter known as "California leather dollars."

In 1841 Governor Juan Alvarado granted land to Andres Duarte just to the east, and the boundary was disputed between Reid's property and Duarte's Rancho Azusa. Don Ygnacio Palomares of the Rancho San Jose farther east, acted as peacemaker. Duarte's adobe home is gone, but you can visit the Palomares adobe in Pomona.

In 1875, much of Reid's land was bought by E.J. "Lucky" Baldwin, a native of Ohio and a shrewd investor in everything Californian: mines, land, ranching, wine, horses. When he paid $200,000 to Harris Newmark and his associates for 8,500 acres of Rancho Santa Anita, it was the largest real estate transaction recorded in Los Angeles to that time.

Baldwin changed the Reid adobe greatly, adding a wood-frame wing. In time, after his death, 111 acres at the heart of the old ranch became the State and County Arboretum in 1947. The central buildings of the property (the Queen Anne Cottage, the Coach Barn, and the Reid/Baldwin home) were all in disrepair but obviously gems of history.

A restoration committee decided to remove the wood additions and rebuild the adobe like Reid's original. More than 15,000 adobe bricks were made, from earth on that spot, for the building and courtyard walls. Wood beams, lintels and thresholds were hand hewn. A new roof was laid of arondo cane. The reconstruction was complete in 1961.

Today you'll find three simple rooms. You won't go in, but through large glass insets you can look into two bedrooms and a central room for dining. The furnishings show mid-19th century rancho life, its simplicity and its few luxuries. Cooking was mainly done outdoors, near the well and ovens. In the earthen courtyard, the days of Reid seem alive again.

How to get there: The Arboretum is at 301 N. Baldwin Ave. From the 210 Freeway, exit at Baldwin and drive south. Call (626) 821-3222.

Tallac Knoll at the
Los Angeles County Arboretum
✧ *Arcadia* ✧

ONE OF THESE CLEAR winter days, make a visit to Tallac Knoll, a historic and beautiful view point in Arcadia at the Arboretum of Los Angeles County.

Below this gentle summit lie the lands which were once the pride of Elias Jackson Baldwin (known as "Lucky".) To the north, some days in startling clarity, are the San Gabriel Mountains.

This area was once the sweeping Santa Anita Rancho. Baldwin, a millionaire from his mining and property interests, bought a part of the ranch in 1875. He eventually owned about 46,000 acres in the San Gabriel Valley, but he especially developed this land where the Arboretum stands today.

Marvelling at Baldwin's estate, a Los Angeles newspaper wrote in 1893, "the soil is as rich as guano and as black as your hat. It will produce anything under the sun." On the rancho Baldwin raised 500 acres of orange groves, 3,000 English walnut trees, orchards of peaches, lemons, apricots and many other fruits.

His vineyards produced 384,000 gallons of wine yearly at their peak. Sheep, cattle, and his famous racing thoroughbreds were abundant too.

Baldwin also operated the Mount Tallac Hotel at Lake Tahoe, with a view of that mountain, and he gave the same name to the scenic hill at his ranch. Tallac Knoll was formed by the Raymond Fault, which also left its scarp across Henry Huntington's estate to the west.

Tallac Knoll had beautiful stands of the native mesa oak, and these remain almost unchanged today. For a time after Lucky Baldwin's death in 1909, his heirs had a piggery at the foot of the knoll, which was casually called Pig Hill.

In 1945, Dr. Samuel Ayres, a Los Angeles horticulturist, came out to see the Baldwin ranch lands as a possible site for a Southern California arboretum and public garden. "This is it," he felt at once. But on top of Tallac Knoll he found a real estate office, with tract maps drawn—the land was about to go on sale.

"This could be the Kew Gardens [London] of the West," said a supporter, and so 111 acres of the old ranch were purchased by the state and county together, for today's Arboretum.

As you stroll along the road curving up the knoll, you'll pass under the oak forest and reach the summit, where an enormous sycamore fig tree presides. This anchors a garden of plants mentioned in the Bible. Elsewhere on the knoll is an appealing jumble of ponds, evergreens, sub-tropicals, and rare trees, some dating to Baldwin's day.

Follow any path to the west of the summit and you'll come to a secluded natural hollow, a hidden and mysterious spot. No one knows for certain what caused this strange dip. Later, after admiring the mountain view, you can leave historic Tallac Knoll on the path descending north, beside a man-made and tree-shaded waterfall.

How to get there: The Arboretum is at 301 N. Baldwin Ave. From the 210 Freeway, exit at Baldwin and drive south. Call (626) 821-3222.

Duarte Historical Museum

✧ *Duarte* ✧

WHERE HAVE THEY BEEN, or even more interesting, what have they been, these historical museums of the San Gabriel Valley? Odd questions perhaps, but consider the good fate of the Duarte Historical Museum.

This trim bungalow, now at rest in Duarte's Encanto Park, has been on its way here for about 70 years. A descendant of the original owners, the Fitts family, tells that it was built in Pasadena and moved sometime in the 1930s to Royal Oaks Drive in Duarte, surrounded by the family's lemon groves.

Later owned by the Mormon Church, it was eventually unwanted and about to be razed. Fortunately, the city of Duarte acquired it for their historical museum and moved it yet again, to the park.

The wanderings of the Fitts house are now over, but history never stands still. In these homelike rooms you will find photographs, mementos, maps, and objects covering the broad estate granted to Andres Duarte in 1841.

All our favorite Southern California themes are here: the beautiful geography of river and mountains, with the San Gabriel River rushing down from the range above; the early rancho days; Big Red Cars crossing the river bridged at Duarte by Henry Huntington; the citrus industry; social tennis of the 1920s, and finally the modern city, declaring independence from its sister Azusa.

But this is not the only historical museum that began as something else. Other transformations have created the Alhambra Historical Museum, a former medical office building donated by its physician-owner, and Monrovia Historical Museum, once the city's municipal plunge. The pool is now replaced by a rose patio and the dressing rooms hold exhibits.

One of our best local museums is the El Monte Historical Museum, formerly the town's library. It was a WPA (Works Progress Administration) project of the 1930s, handsome and built to last. Simpler is the little Meridian Iron Works in South Pasadena, an 1880s wood structure, used as store, chapel, school and iron foundry in its long life. Now it holds South Pasadena history.

Fine architecture is not needed. History-savers need ample space even more. A former telephone building works well for the Whittier Museum, with room to expand. And what about our old train stations, set adrift as train service is cut back? Many ingenious uses have been made of these. In San Dimas, the bright yellow depot holds the Historical Society exhibits and the Pacific Railroad Society.

Pasadena history has its Fenyes Mansion, and Azusa its Durrell House—both are house museums of different kinds. In Glendora, the former firehouse and jail make a historical museum.

Adaptive re-use has brought together historic buildings and museum needs in creative ways. May such happy marriages continue and more be found.

To contact these museums, consult phone directories or inquire at the Duarte Historical Museum for their brochure listing 27 local museums of the San Gabriel Valley.

How to get there: The Duarte Museum is at 777 Encanto Parkway. From the 605 Freeway, exit on Huntington Dr., travel east to Encanto, then north to the museum. Call (626) 357-9419.

Alosta Lost

✧ *Glendora* ✧

"GLENDORA IS A POEM in pepper trees," wrote Joaquin Miller, author and celebrator of the West, in 1908. By that time, the dust had long settled in a classic rivalry of two fledgling towns in the 1880s land boom. Glendora is today's "Pride of the Foothills"—its onetime neighbor, Alosta, only a memory and a street name.

In the mid-1880s, Chicago businessman and health-seeker George D. Whitcomb bought 200 acres of foothill land covering today's Glendora. Shrewdly he persuaded officials of the Santa Fe to route their railway line through the town he planned.

After planting several hundred tiny pepper trees, his Glendora Land Company was ready for business. Buyers snapped up 291 lots on the first day of land sales on April 1, 1887. The town newspaper Glendora Signal proudly claimed that year, "The eyes of Pasadena

are upon us." But a newly-hatched rival was soon to chase Whitcomb's success.

Harrison Fuller, who had sold a large property to Whitcomb, had earlier established a post office for the area. He had named it Alosta for his elder daughter, Anna Losta Fuller, later an operatic singer who performed in Europe.

Then came along Major George E. Gard, U.S. Marshall and land speculator, bent upon having a town of his own. Purchasing 320 acres along today's Alosta Avenue, he began his duel with Whitcomb. Glendora's map was filed in the county office on Sept. 22, 1887; Gard filed one for Alosta the next day.

The rivals spurred each other on. Whitcomb created the impressive Hotel Belleview, and Gard his fine Hotel Correll. Whitcomb bragged of Glendora's foothill views, Gard created "Alosta Heights" in the South Hills. Wild claims flew to attract buyers.

But there were other contrasts. Glendora was set up with strict Methodist values of the time. No liquor could be bought, sold, made or consumed in the town. Whitcomb even placed a liquor clause in every property deed. Education and family solidarity were stressed.

Alosta danced to a different drummer. Its hotel had a bar and dance hall. A saloon across the street sold whiskey at 50 cents a pint.

By 1889, the bottom had fallen out of the land boom. Glendora was building a sound base of business and schools, but Alosta's promoters had lost their shirts at the real estate game. Fewer than two dozen residents checked for their mail at Alosta. Weeds and vacant lots there became an embarrassment to Glendora.

Soon Gard departed, and spunky little Alosta, like many another boomtown, died away. Today Azusa Pacific University occupies the Fuller property where Anna Losta grew up. Alosta Avenue is a ribbon of businesses along the South Hills of Glendora (it is now called "Route 66 – formerly Alosta Avenue"!)

The Glendora Historical Society Museum, in a 1913 building once the city hall, jail, and fire house, displays an early town plan for Alosta.

How to get there: The Glendora Museum is at 314 N. Glendora Ave. Exit the 210 Freeway at Grand Ave., go north to Alosta Ave., turn right, then left on Glendora Ave. Call (626) 963-0419.

Glendora Obelisk of History

✧ *Glendora* ✧

YES, IT DOES LOOK FAMILIAR. In fact, at 10 feet high and 18 square inches at the base, Glendora's obelisk is a miniature replica of the Washington Monument.

The obelisk in front of City Hall was dedicated on the 50th anniversary of Glendora's incorporation as a city: September 30, 1961. Inside a time capsule contains documents and memoirs of the city's history. The capsule is to be opened every 50 years and additions will be made.

Glendora's history goes back to 1868, when two boyhood friends who had served in the Confederate Army came to homestead. John Bender and William Bryant Cullen were from Memphis, Tenn. Their names are honored in street names today, where they once planted wheat and barley, grapevines and orchards.

The main founding father arrived in 1865. George Whitcomb of Chicago came to Southern California for his health and stayed to plat a new town. He bought 200 acres at $40 per acre and persuaded the Santa

Fe Railroad to run its Pasadena-San Bernardino line north of the South Hills, next to his community.

He combined the "glen" of his pleasant valley with his wife's name, Leadora, creating a melodious name for his town. By April 1887, the first public sale of lots was held. The first one sold was on the northeast corner of Bennett and Glendora Avenues, marked today by an inscribed stone.

And what historic events might be noted under the miniature obelisk? The documents may tell about the first citrus packing house in 1896, or the arrivals of telephone service in 1902, the Pacific Electric railway in 1907, and electric power to homes in 1908.

In 1911, the city was incorporated with an area of 2.5 square miles. Its first City Hall (plus jail and fire department) was on Glendora Avenue just north of Bennett Avenue. The building is now the Glendora Historical Museum. The present City Hall was built in 1921 at Foothill Boulevard and Glendora Avenue.

The time capsule must also tell about the 50th anniversary of Glendora's founding. Citizens held a "Golden Get-Together" in 1937, and probably the speeches, photographs of the parade, and historical play performed that day are tucked under the obelisk.

When the obelisk was dedicated, Glendora's citrus groves were almost gone. The population had surged from 4,000 in 1950 to 22,000 in 1961. Soon after the time capsule was sealed up, the Foothill Freeway (210) reached Glendora in 1969.

What's tantalizing about time capsules is that you know they hold fascinating things — the stuff of history — but you can't look until the appointed time. You have to wait.

It's a surprise left for our children and grandchildren, and we may not be here to see what they think of it. In the meantime, this is a pretty obelisk and one of a kind, in Glendora, still the Pride of the Foothills.

How to get there: The Glendora City Hall is on Foothill Blvd. at Glendora Ave. From the 210 Freeway, exit at Grand Ave. and drive north. Turn right on Foothill Blvd. The Glendora Historical Society is nearby at 314 N. Glendora Ave. Call them at (626) 963-0419.

Eaton Canyon County Park
◇ *Pasadena* ◇

YOU CAN WALK in the footsteps of John Muir, the famous naturalist, without scaling a Sierra peak or crossing an Alaskan glacier. Just mosey through picturesque Eaton Canyon County Park, near the eastern border of Pasadena, along its pleasant maze of pathways.

In August of 1877, John Muir made his first visit to Southern California. He was 39 years old, not yet married, and always enjoying "anyplace that's wild." He had come to Pasadena to visit his friend Dr. O. H. Conger, who lived on 30 acres at the corner of Orange Grove Ave. and Colorado Blvd. Pasadena was just a village then, with some 60 families and a checkerboard of orange groves.

Muir admired the town's backdrop of the San Gabriel Mountains. Taking his usual provisions of bread and tea, he set out to explore. He walked first to the mouth of Eaton Canyon as an entrance into the range. There he camped overnight with a solitary water prospector, then continued upward. Pausing at Eaton Falls, he wrote that it was a "charming little poem of wildness."

Beyond the falls, he enjoyed the summer blooms of the native plants: like "a vast bee-pasture." After five days of roaming among the peaks near Mt. Wilson, he descended and returned to his hosts in Pasadena.

Today more than a century of winter rains and summer sun have erased the actual footsteps of John Muir. But you can still follow his route along the seasonal stream of Eaton Canyon County Park. Visit the waterfall, or sit under a weathered oak for a while to read a book of nature or California history. Even studying for an exam would be a satisfying pastime here.

The canyon is named for Judge Benjamin S. Eaton of Pasadena, a native of Connecticut who came to Los Angeles in 1852. His ranch, called Fair Oaks, was just south of the steep gorge now bearing his name. The canyon emerges from the San Gabriel Mountains, then widens into an oak-dotted flood plain. These lands were homesteaded in the 19th century, and parts of the canyon were planted with grapes, barley, and fruit trees.

The present County Park contains 184 acres, with five miles of nature trails winding gently upwards. The county built a nature center there in 1963, and it served school children, the Sierra Club, the Audubon Society, and visitors for many years. But the building was destroyed in the 1993 Altadena fire.

Then a new and finer nature center was dedicated in November 1998. It's a handsome rustic complex in Craftsman style, with a large meeting room, classrooms, live creatures, and fun exhibits to test your knowledge.

The center offers a well-stocked shop of nature books and gifts, native plant gardens, and many programs such as school visits, birdwalks and moonlight hikes. Eaton Canyon is threaded with history, and those footsteps up ahead (across the years) are John Muir's.

How to get there: Eaton Canyon County Park is at 1750 N. Altadena Dr. From the Foothill (210) Freeway, exit at Altadena Dr. and drive north. Call (626) 398-5420.

Finnish Folk Art Museum
✧ *Pasadena* ✧

FINLAND IS ALMOST the same length and width as California, although a third of the country lies north of the Arctic Circle. Still more than half covered by forests of pine, spruce and birch, this beautiful land has a long and distinctive culture of rural life. You can step into this faraway world for a moment at the Finnish Folk Art Museum in Pasadena.

This exhibit, rare outside of Finland, is on the grounds of the Pasadena Museum of History. The Fenyes mansion there was built in 1905 by the grandmother of Mrs. Y.A. Paloheimo, wife of the

Finnish consul in the southwestern United States from 1947 to 1965.

As a native of Jarvenpaa, Finland (also home of the composer Jean Sibelius), Consul Paloheimo wanted to establish a tribute to Finnish-Americans and to show the domestic arts of his homeland. In 1949 he bought the little redwood structure, modeled after a Swiss chalet, which noted architect Frederick Roehrig had designed as a garage for an Orange Grove Boule-

22

vard estate. Paloheimo moved the building to its present location, using it first as a guest house.

The Industrial Revolution did not touch the Finnish countryside until the 20th century, so Paloheimo found many handmade articles as he visited self-sustaining farm families in his travels. Together with the Finlandia Foundation, the Pasadena Museum of History has created a model of a peasant home, now filled with useful and decorative objects.

The snug living room contains an open hearth for cooking and heating, and a double-decker bed hung with bright colored textiles. Woodcraft and woven arts predominate, using the country's resources of forests, flax and wool. Many items are traditional gifts: the carved chairs given by farmers to their daughters as brides, the cradle given by a father to his wife for their firstborn.

There are no museum labels, as this represents a home. The poles hanging from the ceiling were for storing bread, baked with a center hole. The reindeer horn object is a candlestick; a moose skin bag was for hunting.

Households like this show a culture artfully using what was at hand. Made from the ever-present birch bark, there are boxes, a ladle, rope, a knapsack, a shepherd's horn and even woven slippers. The peaceful interior has a certain aroma, perhaps from all the wood.

A second room features "rya" rugs, the best known of Finnish woven goods. One is about 200 years old, a deep blue with border of symbolic motifs, made with natural dyes. Several large photographs show the Finnish countryside, mainly forests and water (the country's Finnish name, Suomi, means marshland). A third of the room is the traditional sauna, the dry heat bath which Finns alternate with a bracing dip in a cold lake or shower, or even in the snow.

The Finnish Museum is open only by prior arrangement. Call to inquire.

How to get there: The Pasadena Museum of History is at 470 W. Walnut St., at the corner of Orange Grove Blvd. From the 210 Freeway, exit at Orange Grove, drive north and turn right on Walnut. Call (626) 577-1660.

Fuller Theological Seminary
◇ *Pasadena* ◇

A WALK THROUGH the campus of Fuller Theological Seminary will take you among the buildings of noted Pasadena architects, and into the turn-of-the-century tract known as Ford Place. A walking tour leaflet, created for the school's 50th anniversary in 1997, provides architectural notes and history.

The school was founded by Charles Fuller, who was raised in Redlands where his father grew Fuller's Fancy Oranges. After graduating from Pomona College in 1910, he managed Placentia's largest fruit packing house before becoming a minister.

In 1947, he founded his non-denominational seminary, first occupying the Craven estate on South Orange Grove Boulevard which now houses the American Red Cross.

In 1963, the school and its 250 students settled on the present campus on North Oakland Avenue. That year Payton Hall was built for administration and named for Fuller's father-in-law. The Gothic

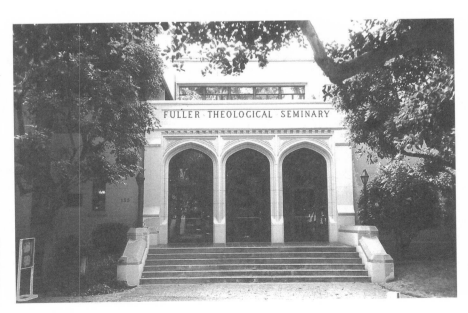

design includes three unusual arched plate glass doors, and a pleasing scale to fit into its surroundings.

The seminary developed in a historic residential district, which they would preserve and enhance over the years. In the 1970s, Oakland Avenue was closed for one block and replaced by a grassy walkway among knolls and trees.

The northern part of the 11-acre campus was Ford Place, an elegant subdivision of homes established in 1900 by Todd Ford Sr., a major stockholder in the Pasadena Ice Company. His fortune from ice allowed for a beautiful development.

The homes on Ford Place acquired for the Fuller campus had been designed by Sylvanus B. Marston, Frederick Roehrig, C.W. Buchanan, and Charles and Henry Greene—all major names from California architectural history.

These substantial houses of Ford Place and Oakland Avenue, with their gables, verandas, and distinct personalities, now hold the offices and academic programs of a busy seminary. Without cars, the atmosphere of your walk is serene and even studious, ideal for enjoying the varied architecture.

Just north of the Fuller-owned buildings is the Blinn House, built in 1905 and now the Women's City Club. This is an example of Prairie architecture, designed by George Maher, who was a colleague of Frank Lloyd Wright in Chicago. It is part of the original Ford Place.

To savor this walk, with historical notes on both the seminary and the neighborhood, ask at Fuller's Public Relations Office for the tour leaflet or other information. Two beautiful Pasadena museums are also within a block of this campus: the Pacific Asia Museum at 46 N. Los Robles Ave. (626) 449-2742, and the new Pasadena Museum of California Art at 490 E. Union St. (626) 568-3665. One is a Chinese palace and the other a striking modern design. Combine one or both of these with your campus walk and you will see a rather amazing spectrum of Pasadena architecture and style.

How to get there: Fuller Theological Seminary is at 135 N. Oakland Ave. From the 210 Freeway, exit at Lake Ave. and drive south; turn right on Union St. to Oakland. Call the seminary at (626) 584-5200.

Gamble House
◇ *Pasadena* ◇

IF THE ROLLING LAWNS were swells on a gentle sea, Pasadena's Gamble House would be a well-timbered ship with its rafters firm to a steady breeze. There is something ship-like about this "ultimate bungalow," designed by Charles and Henry Greene. Its snug woodwork and harmonizing furniture seem to define the term "shipshape."

The Greene brothers were born just outside Cincinnati, Ohio, 15 months apart. Both studied architecture at the Massachusetts Institute of Technology. When their parents moved to Pasadena, Charles and Henry joined them in 1893. On the way west, they visited the World's Columbian Exposition in Chicago and were impressed by the Japanese architecture there.

Pasadena was then a small town less than 20 years old, but already it was attracting prosperous citizens. The Greenes worked in traditional styles, then started on their own distinctive path. They designed houses for the California climate and environment, using

common materials of brick, stone and wood. "Why disguise them?" wrote Charles Greene. "The noblest work of art is to make these common things beautiful for man."

In 1908, the Greenes began work on their most famous house (pictured here under construction), for David and Mary Gamble of the Procter and Gamble Company. Sited above the Arroyo Seco, the Gamble House is a masterpiece of the Arts and Crafts movement, which valued handwork and fine details. Its construction was of California redwood, Oregon cedar, boulders from the Arroyo, and Pasadena's own bricks.

Outside, the house shows off broad eaves, bands of windows, sleeping porches and terraces. All these features aim to shelter the occupants from fierce sunlight while capturing all possible light and breezes. It was a new vision, truly a Southern California house. You can also see Japanese touches, in the exterior gateways and lanterns.

Inside, hand-rubbed woods glow beside leaded and stained glass. The Greenes designed the furniture, lighting, cabinetry, rugs, and landscaping, even downspouts and light switches. The satiny woodwork makes a strong impression. Docents tell us that later buyers were considering painting the interior white, so the Gamble heirs, horrified, canceled that sale and presented the house to the City of Pasadena.

"Doors should be interesting in themselves and not merely holes of entrance and exit," declared Charles Greene. Few doors have met this aim like the glorious Oak Tree entrance doors made for the Gamble House by the Tiffany Studios in New York. Copper foil wraps each piece of colored glass in the overall design.

Now the house is administered by the city, while the University of Southern California School of Architecture offers education and preservation programs there. Tours are conducted through the house, and visitors may browse in a bookstore devoted to art, architecture and Pasadena, in the Gamble House garage (a choice little Craftsman building itself). Also, you can pick up a self-guided walking tour leaflet for the surrounding neighborhood, to explore the context of this famous house.

How to get there: The Gamble House is at 300 N. Orange Grove Blvd. From the 210 Freeway, exit at Orange Grove and drive north. Before you visit, call (626) 793-3334.

Hotel Green
✧ *Pasadena* ✧

ALL THE EARLY Southern California communities had their hotels and boarding houses, as various settlers arrived in town. But the grand resort hotels – now that was another matter. In their prime, a handful of these establishments became social meccas, visited by U.S. presidents and other notables. Pasadena had a lion's share of them, and none was more colorful than that Moorish fantasy, the Hotel Green.

The hotel was built in stages, starting in 1886 on the east side of Raymond Avenue (a building now gone). Colonel C.C. Green of New Jersey was a winter visitor to Pasadena with a fortune from patent medicines such as "Green's August Flower" and "Green's Ague Conqueror." He invested in the fledgling hotel, built himself a house in Altadena, and named his daughter Altadena too.

The six-story annex to Col. Green's hotel was designed by Frederick Roehrig and built in 1898 on the west side of Raymond, with a covered bridge to the original building. This very large structure and part of the bridge survive today.

In 1899, more than 1,000 guests danced at the formal opening of this West Annex, strolling on the roof-garden and exploring the elegant parlors. The stucco exterior included high turrets and two round towers facing Central Park. Each level within the towers contains a beautiful round living room.

Wildly eclectic, the building boasted a Mediterranean sun room, grand Victorian lobby, Turkish and Moorish reception rooms with hand-wrought woodwork, a marble staircase, gracious ballroom and a veranda straight from the Indian Raj. Outside, intricate bands of gold decorated the walls, and many windows caught the light. All this splendor among the palm trees is basically unchanged today.

The new building carried on the honor of the Hotel Green, which had already welcomed President Benjamin Harrison as a guest in 1891 and hosted a banquet for Professor Thaddeus Lowe on completion of his incline railroad to Echo Mountain in 1893.

In 1924, a group of winter visitors from the Midwest and East bought the West Annex. Renamed the Castle Green, it became 50 individually-owned apartments in one of the first co-op buildings in the United States. The ballroom and first floor parlors were, and still are, shared by all the residents.

Time and luck have been kind to the Castle Green. Now listed on the National Register of Historic Places, it has been restored through a $700,000 grant in recent years. Seismic engineers and other experts have gone over it with a fine-toothed comb. Still, the care of this centenarian will always be a challenge.

The Castle Green holds a Holiday Tour each December, and its large rather amazing parlors are available for weddings and events. All the funds raised go to the preservation of the building. You will be able to see this gem of history for yourself, on these special occasions.

How to get there: The Castle Green (Hotel Green) is at 99 S. Raymond Ave., just south of the Old Pasadena district. From the 210 Freeway, exit at Orange Grove Blvd. and drive south. Turn left on Green St. and right on Raymond. For information, call (626) 793-0359.

La Pintoresca Library and Park

✧ *Pasadena* ✧

YOU CAN SAY you're going up to "La Pint" (that rhymes with "mint"), for such is the modern nickname of a busy branch library and park in north Pasadena. The spot is La Pintoresca, meaning "the picturesque," and it holds more than 100 years of Pasadena history.

Imagine the view from this slope in 1888, over a valley filled with fruit groves in young Pasadena below. That year John H. Painter and his sons built an 85-room hotel (later expanded to 100 rooms) on 32 acres.

The Painter Hotel, on Washington Boulevard between Fair Oaks and Raymond Avenue, had an excellent wine cellar and a broad veranda. A special horsecar line brought guests up from the town center below.

The hotel was later renamed La Pintoresca, but in 1912 it burned down. The city purchased the beautiful grounds in 1914 and made them a park.

Meanwhile, the seeds of a library for the neighborhood were sprouting. The Woman's Christian Temperance Union (WCTU) opened a reading room in 1905 in the basement of the Methodist Church nearby. Later, they used a local store. Then in 1908 the project became the north Pasadena branch of the city's public library.

The present distinctive building, designed by architects Bennett and Haskell, was finished in 1930. Outwardly of Spanish style, it is in the form of a Greek cross (wide arms of equal length) with a striking central space filled with light from high windows.

Each of the reading rooms can be supervised from the center. The main entrance is in an angular space between two of the wings. A club room and exhibition hall complete La Pintoresca Library.

The surroundings of this library and park have changed over the years. The book collections are updated and reflect the ethnic diversity of north Pasadena. School groups have made frequent visits to "La Pint" for years. The meeting room has served the community with such activities as a well-baby clinic, Black History classes, after-school tutors, art workshops and more.

In the last few decades this branch weathered several attempts to close it. Citizens mobilized to preserve it each time. All of our public institutions must be used and appreciated, and sometimes defended, if they are to survive history's twists and turns.

Outside, the park holds bright-colored play equipment and green lawns for active games. Along Washington Boulevard are some great old trees, which must date back to the hotel days.

La Pintoresca Library, which is now designated a Pasadena Cultural Heritage Landmark, is a gem of architecture well worth a visit. It offers a busy summer program with crafts, story hours, puppet shows, and lots of books to intrigue children and adults. Although the historic hotel had just a short life, its shady grounds live on as an asset for the families of Pasadena.

How to get there: The library and park are at 1355 N. Raymond Ave. From the 210 Freeway, exit at Fair Oaks Ave. and drive north. Turn right on Washington Blvd. to the corner of Raymond. Call (626) 744-7268.

Pasadena Central Library

◇ *Pasadena* ◇

"BE MADE WHOLE by books as by great spaces and the stars."

Can you find this inscription, the words of California poet Mary C. Davies, on the front of the central Pasadena Public Library? Don't be in a hurry, because you'll be searching through a feast of symbolic details – books, griffins, faces, and garlands.

All this decorates the stately façade of architect Myron Hunt's 1927 library building, a California interpretation of Mediterranean style. The courtyard fountain was copied from one in Spain's palace-fortress, the Alhambra. Long-legged palms poke up from within the patio walls, like elegant feather dusters.

Pasadena's library goes back to 1882, when developer and visionary Abbot Kinney helped found the Pasadena Library and Village Improvement Society. (He started free public library systems in Santa Monica and Venice too.) Kinney had settled on his east Pasadena ranch, called Kinneloa, and disliked the 15-mile buggy trip to the library in Los Angeles.

The town's first library building was completed in 1890 on Raymond Avenue. Only the entry arches of this early structure remain today at the northwest corner of Memorial Park.

Then in 1925 Myron Hunt, architect of the Huntington Library and Occidental College, won a competition to design a new library. It was the first building finished in a Pasadena Civic Center plan inspired by the City Beautiful Movement. Later, the City Hall and the Civic Auditorium completed the proposed trio.

Hunt's design included the façade with its Renaissance-echoing arches, the 42-foot high Main Hall, and the Peter Pan Room – the children's library named for the carvings on its stone fireplace.

Generations of Pasadenans have come to this library. A survey in the 1980s showed that 61 percent of the city's residents held library cards, an unusually high proportion. But eventually wear and tear threatened the aging building.

Enter the Pasadena Public Library Foundation in 1984, determined to restore and improve the library, now a mother library to eight branches. Their plans called for adding a new public entrance from the north parking lot, replacing the two-level book stack with four levels, and adding a new online book catalog with 16 miles of cable throughout the building.

All this, and also keeping the new materials as close to the originals as possible: the Portuguese cork floor was renewed in the Main Hall, the lighting fixtures and furniture either restored or replicated, and the oak paneling refinished.

The success of this $2.4 million project earned the library a 1990 special award from the National Trust for Historic Preservation, one of 15 winners from hundreds of nominees across the country.

To savor this new-yet-old space, have a look for more inscriptions in the Main Hall. You'll find the poet Marlowe's words "Infinite riches in a little room." And perhaps you'll agree with the philosopher Montaigne: "Here I am in my kingdom."

How to get there: The Library is at 285 E. Walnut St. From the 210 Freeway, exit at Lake Ave. and drive south. Turn right on Walnut. For information, call (626) 744-4052.

Pasadena City College Observatory
✧ *Pasadena* ✧

IT WAS ONE of those bright February days, and a crowd of some 8,000 people had gathered around a picturesque little building in Pasadena. Around it were garden plots and open fields; clear in the distance lay the San Gabriel Mountains.

A revered bushy-haired figure spoke briefly in his native German. The year was 1931, and that was Dr. Albert Einstein, dedicating the new observatory at Pasadena Junior College (now known as Pasadena City College).

The little astronomy building, with its two domes, had been built at a cost of $35,000. It would house two telescopes (20 inches and 9 inches), a lecture classroom, a laboratory for spectroscopy, a transit room and dark rooms. On the flat roof were columns for movable instruments.

The craftsmanship of the time showed in the Mexican tile floors, wrought iron work, and neat miniature stairways curving up to the domes. Over the entrance was a small carving showing Galileo, looking a bit like a wizard, with his telescope.

At the ceremony, John Harbeson, principal of the college, read a translation of Einstein's speech which began: "My dear young people, I am glad to see you this day, happy youth of this sunny and blest land."

Dr. Walter Adams, director of the Mount Wilson Observatory, praised the college for taking its place in the study of astronomy, alongside Mount Wilson and the California Institute of Technology. A bouquet of flowers for Frau Einstein, a song from the college's Bulldog Band, and the building was officially launched.

"Keep your copy of this issue," urged the college newspaper (the Pasadena Chronicle) the next day, "for it will be a valuable souvenir of the historic event. . . The nation is Einstein-mad, and now the world will know that Pasadena Junior College has a new astronomy building." The people of the Crown City had followed the Einsteins with delight during their eight-week stay hosted by Caltech.

When the distinguished visitors departed by train, college student leaders saw them off with gifts of California fruit and copies of the school yearbook.

Today the vintage building looks just the same, but more miniature than ever next to a massive four-story parking structure. Once in an isolated spot away from the main campus, the observatory is now solidly hemmed in as the college has grown out and surrounded it.

The stars are dimmed now by bright security lights from the parking garage ("That's our super-nova," joked one professor.) But astronomy study here is very much alive. A planetarium wing has been added, often visited by local school groups. A small but strong contingent of PCC students sometimes works with Jet Propulsion Laboratory and Mount Wilson scientists. Computer and machine shop students at the college collaborate with the young astronomers on projects.

And technology has ways now to cut past the interfering lights and reach out to the deep sky beyond.

How to get there: Pasadena City College is at 1570 E. Colorado Blvd. at the corner of Hill Ave. From the 210 Freeway, exit at Hill Ave. and drive south. For information, call (626) 585-7315.

Pasadena Humane Society

✧ *Pasadena* ✧

IN 1932 a new Renaissance Revival building was dedicated in Pasadena, designed by noted architect Robert T. Ainsworth. But something was different: the roof bore an iron weather vane with a dog chasing a cat, for this was the new home of the Pasadena Humane Society, still in the same building today.

The society itself is nearly 100 years old, approaching its centennial. Founded in 1903, it first cared not for pets but for the working animals of the day. Horses were the most overworked of all. The society investigated cruelty as horses hauled sand and gravel from the Arroyo, and they watched over all building projects using horses and mules. In 1903 they also found new homes for 17 dogs and seven cats.

The next year a public water fountain for horses was given to the city by a winter visitor. The marble and bronze fountain still stands, at the northeast corner of Pasadena's Central Park. Soon the society and its supporters installed a dozen others around the city.

Animal hospitals were needed too and in 1907 the society set up several, with a new horse-drawn ambulance to carry the sick or injured horses.

From its origins until the mid-1930s, the Pasadena Humane Society also rescued and found homes for children. This was a smaller part of its work (in 1908, for example, they handled 130 human cases and 1,243 animal cases), but it was important, as there were no other children's services in that time. The society's earliest logo shows a dog and a child, both to be protected.

As Pasadena grew, so did the need for animal care. The society first had an office in the old City Hall, with its animals kept near the city barn. By 1909 they were beginning to lease and acquire property on Raymond Avenue, still their current home.

Public support has always been strong, and during the Depression they were able to build the elegant and practical building designed by Ainsworth. Its symmetrical façade and twin arches are highlighted by wrought iron details of animals. The unusual walls are Lockstone, pre-cast cement slabs that appear to be stone masonry.

One archway leads to the ample kennel areas behind the building. Also at the back is a simple two-story garage and apartment, designed in 1929 by Myron Hunt and H.C. Chambers.

The newest building, completed in 1994, harmonizes beautifully with the historic architecture and holds a clinic, a small auditorium, dog kennels and cat ward, and two adoption counseling rooms. The whole complex now has state-of-the-art accommodations serving Pasadena, South Pasadena, San Marino, Sierra Madre, Arcadia, and La Canada Flintridge.

In a recent year the society found new homes for 1,658 dogs and 1,279 cats, thanks to about 350 devoted volunteers. This is one landmark building that can truly be described as "full of life."

How to get there: The Humane Society is at 361 S. Raymond Ave. From the 210 Freeway, exit at Lake Ave. and drive south to Del Mar Ave. Turn right, then left on Raymond. Call (626) 792-7151.

Pasadena Labor Temple
✧ *Pasadena* ✧

THE GREAT DEPRESSION crept over Pasadena like the familiar marine layer of clouds, dampening a city of comfortable wealth and changing the dynamics of everything. But as the economy faltered, a dream of 20 years was actually coming true: the building of the sturdy brick Labor Temple, completed in 1931.

In 1911 the Pasadena Union Labor Temple Association was formed, to bring organized labor its own home in the city. They purchased land at the corner of Raymond and Walnut Streets, and the unions met in five old houses on the property. For many years they saved and planned.

In August 1931, excavation began for the Temple, with all dirt taken out by hand. The building was raised with union labor at a time when work was urgently needed. All the crafts took part, from brickwork to plastering, plumbing and carpentry.

With pride the Pasadena workers extended fraternal greetings to the State Federation of Labor, inviting all to visit the completed Temple. They hoped that someday organized labor would have its own newspaper in Pasadena, to extend the message of progress.

The City Directory of Pasadena in 1932 (these volumes are a wonderful "slice of life" of the city) lists 20 labor organizations, from Barbers to the Women's Union Label League. These locals were mostly of the building trades, and three were specifically women's groups. All were listed as meeting in the new Labor Temple.

This is a simple brick building, originally one story with a second story added in 1953. It is a "temple" because of the honor and dignity of its function. A few classical touches plus ornamental ironwork grace the façade. The interior steps have colorful Spanish-style tiles. The words "Labor Temple" are carved in the lintel over the entrance. The building has a solid utilitarian air, but decoration was not forgotten.

The labor movement grew in that era and kept its place in civic life for many years. But in the 1990s, the Labor Temple held just one labor union office, plus other businesses. The building was becoming isolated in an area facing redevelopment.

Today the restored building is linked to a newly constructed five-story senior housing project next door, connected by corridors. The Temple holds 15 of the 70 apartment units, and its main meeting room is now the project's community room.

The housing is close to Memorial Park and to Old Pasadena, and it makes an adaptive re-use of the landmark once created with such pride and spirit. The Temple is listed in the National Register of Historic Places.

And in 1995, the City of Pasadena added the Temple's 8-foot sign to its Historic Sign Inventory. This list includes signs installed before 1960 which exemplify the craftsmanship and design of their period. Today the Labor Temple sign shows up as proudly as ever, no doubt provoking curiosity about what the building may be now. Inside, the urban mini-temple holds respectful housing for those who have finished their working years.

How to get there: The Temple is at 42 E. Walnut St. From the 210 Freeway, exit at Orange Grove Blvd., and drive north, then right on Walnut.

Pasadena Post Office

✧ *Pasadena* ✧

THE PASADENA CIVIC CENTER DISTRICT, a constellation of beautiful civic buildings, was placed on the National Register of Historic Places in 1980. But did you know that the oldest building of that group is the U.S. Postal Service office on Colorado Boulevard? Today its handsome arches are directly across from the Paseo Colorado, Pasadena's new shopping and living complex.

This Post Office must have held a proud dominance when it was completed in 1915. Its style has been called Italian Renaissance Revival, but also "American Renaissance" with a touch of Southern California in its white plaster walls and red tile roof. Five pairs of iron grilled gates and the iron balconies on the second floor give it a Mediterranean feel. But architect Oscar Wenderoth also created an entrance loggia with arches reminiscent of the California missions.

This formal public building was featured in a 1918 issue of "Western Architect," a leading architectural periodical of its time, published in Chicago. They praised its white marble base and graceful steps, which were originally white marble too but are now of a fine red granite for easier footing.

Inside, the main hall is like the courtyard of a Renaissance palace, covered with a skylight of patterned colored glass. The many arched doorways are trimmed with terra cotta reliefs of cream and honey coloring, with vivid blues. Decorative bands encircle the space with restrained richness. You'll find the Great Seal of the United States and also of the State of California. The columns have American eagles and the ornamental metal work has fine touches rarely seen today.

In 1939, an addition was built to the north, designed by Sylvanus Marston. This simpler wing is quite harmonious with the older structure in material and proportions.

Nearby is Pasadena's Civic Center, designed by the Chicago planning firm of Bennett, Parsons and Frost in the "City Beautiful" style of the 1920s. The three major buildings there are City Hall (1926), the Public Library to the north (1925), and the Civic Auditorium to the south (completed in 1932). When this distinguished trio was built, the Post Office was already in its place, as were the YWCA (1920) and the YMCA (1910 and 1925). Today all these structures are honored together on the National Register.

Several years ago, the Post Office enjoyed a seismic retrofit for earthquake safety, and a renovation of its well-aged interior. Today it is actively used by the public, and its second floor contains postal inspection services.

This is one of the beautiful interior spaces of Pasadena. So after shopping or lunch at the new Paseo, step across the street and enjoy the surprise.

How to get there: The Post Office is at 281 E. Colorado Blvd. (the northwest corner of Colorado Blvd. and Garfield Ave.) From the 210 Freeway, exit at Lake Ave. and drive south; turn right on Colorado.

St. Andrew's Church
✧ *Pasadena* ✧

THE FAMILIAR 140-foot brick belltower soars above the 210 Freeway, assuring traveling Pasadenans that yes, they have returned home. But the magnificent church at the foot of the tower is a rarity that everyone will enjoy. It seems that you have stepped into Italy.

This is St. Andrew's Catholic Church, a Romanesque masterpiece begun in 1928. Its inspiration is several medieval churches of Rome with their timeless beauty: the Basilica of Santa Sabina for the interior and Santa Maria in Cosmedin for the façade and bell tower.

This parish began when some 400 Catholics living around Pasadena in 1885 needed a church home. The nearest Mass for them was the San Gabriel Mission, the Old Plaza Church or the Cathedral in Los Angeles. Their first St. Andrew's Church was a simple frame structure like a schoolhouse topped with a cross, on Pasadena Avenue at Bellefontaine.

From 1899 to 1927, the parish enjoyed a new brick building at Fair Oaks and Walnut. During that time, the parish school, Holy Names Academy, bought the nearby Throop Polytechnic Hall, where Caltech

(California Institute of Technology) had its start. So did the paths of these two Pasadena institutions cross in the early 1920s. The old Throop served the parish until the new church school was built in 1949.

In its formative years, St. Andrew's had the touch of the Irish, as five of its first seven pastors were alumni of All Hallows College, Dublin, Ireland. One of the Irish priests, Monsignor McCarthy, claimed as his own the Fighting Irish of Notre Dame, including Knute Rockne and the Four Horsemen, when they arrived for the 1925 Rose Bowl game against Stanford. Following Mass and a sprinkling of holy water, the Fighting Irish carried the day.

When the growing congregation needed a larger home, architect Ross Montgomery traveled to Rome for inspiration. A recent restoration, lasting several years, has brought back the original splendor he designed for St. Andrew's.

Go on a bright day if you can, for the windows are high and small, though richly hued. The church nave is an amazingly long and tall space, with a final dome of Venetian gold mosaic. The 40-foot high altar canopy is a wedding cake of layers and little columns.

Twenty-four massive multi-colored columns pace the length of the church, apparently different kinds of marble. But these are actually stucco covered with a marbleizing technique called "scagliola," a coating of gypsum, glue and marble dust. This method of illusion was developed by 17th and 18th century Germans who did not have marble at hand.

Candles glow before niches and side chapels. Twelve elegant hanging lights are massive yet airy, made of metal filagree. From outside, the faint hum of traffic seems to reinforce the sense of shelter within. And yet this is no medieval sanctuary but a busy modern-day parish of Spanish and English-speaking families, with a welcome for all.

How to get there: The church is at 311 N. Raymond Ave. From the 210 Freeway, exit at Fair Oaks and drive south. Turn left on Chestnut and left on Raymond. Call (626) 792-4183.

Tournament Park and the Vin Fiz
✧ *Pasadena* ✧

YOU NEED TO HEAR this story. Then you'll know about the Vin Fiz, and why a piece of Pasadena history is in the National Air and Space Museum of the Smithsonian in Washington, D.C.

There was nationwide attention in November 1911 for Pasadena's Tournament Park, which is now the property of Caltech (California Institute of Technology).

In 1901 the Tournament of Roses had bought 14 country acres called Patton Field, from the family of future general George S. Patton. The land was far from the center of town, but ideal for sports events like tug of war, bicycle and running races, polo, and chariot races, with colorful "Romans" driving teams of four horses.

In 1902 they tried football there, and although Michigan defeated Stanford 49-0, a Rose Game tradition was born.

But the grandest adventure was the Vin Fiz, which made the first transcontinental flight across the U.S., from Long Island to Pasadena.

William Randolph Hearst offered a prize of $50,000 to the first person to fly across this country in 30 days or less before Oct. 10, 1911. Eight years before, the Wright brothers at Kitty Hawk had managed to keep the first power-driven aircraft aloft for only one minute.

Calbraith (Cal) Rodgers, from a family of adventurers, took on this challenge. J. Ogden Armour financed the trip as publicity for his new 5-cent soft drink, Vin Fiz. He also chartered a train to accompany and support the flight.

Rodgers flew a Wright Brothers Model EX biplane, with a 35-horsepower engine and open cockpit, the frame of wood and piano wire covered with fabric airfoil. Its two propellers were driven by bicycle chains, and its gross weight was 903 pounds.

The gas tank held 15 gallons, enough for 3 1/2 hours, and the plane had only one speed: wide open. It was airborne in 75 feet.

Cal was a novice, but everyone was in those days. After six 15-minute lessons, he was soloing. The support train carried spare parts, more than enough for two complete planes plus two extra engines. They needed it all.

Rodgers followed railroad tracks west, as his "iron compass." Averaging 88 miles per day (with many down days for weather and repairs), he reached Pasadena after 68 hops and 15 crashes in 49 days. Thousands saw him land in this park, with some fancy spirals and a maneuver called a "Texas Tommy."

Alas, Hearst kept the prize money, as Rodgers had only reached Oklahoma when the deadline passed. But Rodgers banqueted, a hero, at Pasadena's Maryland Hotel.

So that is why the Vin Fiz is in the Smithsonian, with its more famous sisters, the Spirit of St. Louis and the Gossamer Albatross.

Today, the Tournament of Roses is at the Rose Bowl, the old Patton Field has become Caltech's playing fields, and only a little green playground remains as Tournament Park. It's a fine spot for children's picnics, and do tell them the story of the Vin Fiz.

How to get there: The park entrance is off Wilson Ave. between California and Arden. From the 210 Freeway, exit at Hill Ave., drive south, turn right on California and left on Wilson.

Westminster Presbyterian Church
✧ *Pasadena* ✧

"SERVICES WILL BE HELD wherever the church building is on Sunday morning," said the Rev. William Dodge, first senior pastor of the present-day Westminster Presbyterian Church in Pasadena. But that year was 1908, and the "movable" church was a little redwood chapel, being pulled to a new site by mule teams (a journey taking several weeks).

The congregation had started out as the Lake Avenue Mission Branch of the Pasadena Presbyterian Church. For six months they worshipped in the picturesque wooden church at Lake Avenue and Claremont Street, then purchased the site they occupy to this day.

Rains complicated the move, and the streetcar line on Lake Avenue made that route impossible. So the building traveled up Catalina Avenue. When the church was settled and landscaped at Lake and Woodbury, the congregation entered a photograph of it in a Ladies Home Journal design contest, where it won first place for a bungalow church.

In 1916, the architect Sylvanus Marston designed a new and

larger sanctuary for the property. By this time, the congregation was independent from its "mother church" and growing well beyond its original 51 members.

Both these buildings still stood in 1928 when Westminster Presbyterian dedicated its present and grandest sanctuary: the French Gothic church now lifting its crowned tower 150 feet above Lake Avenue. The architects were Marston and Maybury. California Governor C.C. Young spoke at the laying of the cornerstone.

The structure is of reinforced concrete, with pointed arched windows and a slate roof. Inside, the church is impressively high, with rare painted ceilings of blue or red plaster sprinkled with stars, giving a Byzantine look.

Sunlight glows in three large rose windows, with richly colored panes set in Gothic tracery. These are known as the Sapphire, Emerald, and Ruby Windows. Done in the "grisaille style" of the 13th century, they were designed and made at the Judson Studios of Los Angeles. Above the white marble communion table is the tall and brilliant Christ window, also by the Judson artists.

In the Sierra Madre Earthquake of 1991, a piece of the tower fell through the roof, dashing the starry ceiling and the pews below. Today, you would never know of this disaster, so skillful was the restoration. The church accommodates 1,100 people on its main floor, and the upper galleries are now used for various purposes.

The church's Reuter organ was constructed with 2,678 pipes, but ranks of trumpet pipes will be added to resonate in the Gothic spaces high above.

The little bungalow church and the first Sylvanus Marston sanctuary are no more, removed in 1957 for building of the Morrison Fellowship Hall. But views of the congregation's first home, pulled by the mules (uphill all the way), remain in photographs and in memories.

How to get there: Westminster Presbyterian Church is at 1757 North Lake Avenue. From the 210 Freeway, exit at Lake and drive north. Call (626) 794-7141.

The Mother Vine
✧ *San Gabriel* ✧

THERE'S SOMETHING INTRIGUING about a historic landmark that is a plant. After all, it's alive and this one has cast its offspring around the world, becoming known as "the mother vine."

It's the old grapevine of San Gabriel, planted around 1861 just west of the Mission. Some accounts gave its planting date as 1775, the year Mission San Gabriel Archangel was established at its present site (having been threatened by floods at its original spot beside the San Gabriel River). But actually the vine dates from the mid-19th century.

One record states that it was a wild grapevine from a canyon near the home of Benjamin D. (Don Benito) Wilson at Lake Vineyard. Wilson's home was near present-day Lacy Park in San Marino, and to the east lay the lands of Leonard J. Rose, a property called Sunnyslope. Rose had been growing the vine, but in 1861 he allowed a settler named David F. Hall to dig up the vine and take it by buggy to his home in San Gabriel.

There the vine grew luxuriously and its shade was used for a summer outdoor kitchen. Near the end of his life, as the grapevine was becoming famous, Hall apparently swore to these origins in a notarized affidavit dated 1908.

Next to the ever-vigorous grapevine was one of the many adobe dwellings that used to cluster around the Mission. This one, now gone, was a home and then an inn. It became known as "Ramona's Birthplace" because Helen Hunt Jackson, author of the novel "Ramona," once stayed there.

Cuttings were taken from the vine over the years and sent to nearby estates and to some of the other missions. In 1946 the vine, which once covered some 10,000 square feet, collapsed of its own weight. It was nursed back to health and continued to produce grapes.

In October 1957, representatives of 18 countries, plus wine growers and city officials, placed a marker at the vine honoring 100 years of California winemaking. The international visitors took back cuttings to plant in their countries, which included Germany, France, Spain, Portugal, Israel, Chile, Austria, Greece, Canada, Mexico, Australia, and more.

Now the vine is surrounded by a little walled city park, next to San Gabriel's Adult Recreation Center. The vine is trimmed every 10 years or so in January, when it is dormant. Today its crown is kept relatively small, but there are new tips and tendrils showing strong signs of life.

Picnic facilities around the historic vine are available by reservation through the City Recreation Department. The Mission is just a stroll away, and to the west is the Mission Playhouse, built in 1927, now called the San Gabriel Civic Auditorium. Find more information about the vine and its surroundings at the San Gabriel Historical Museum, nearby at 546 W. Broadway.

How to get there: The grapevine is at 324 S. Mission Dr. From the 10 Freeway, exit at Del Mar Ave. and drive north. Turn left on Mission Dr. For park information, call (626) 308-2875. The San Gabriel Historical Museum is at (626) 308-3223.

San Gabriel Nursery

✧ *San Gabriel* ✧

THE PURSUIT OF HISTORY may lead to unexpected links, between people and places we thought we knew separately. So it is with the 75-year old San Gabriel Nursery and Florist, one of the oldest nurseries in Southern California.

This thriving resource dates back to the vivacious 1920s, when many estates were being built and landscaped in Pasadena and San Marino. Fred Waichi Yoshimura had come to San Francisco from Yamaguchi, Japan, in 1917 at the age of 21. He settled in San Gabriel, learned gardening and plant propagation, and started his business (then called Mission Nursery) in 1923.

Soon he married Mitoko Naito, also a native of Japan, and she began their florist work, including flower wreaths for horses in the Rose Parade. She also cared for her family's own horses, used by her husband for travel to his gardening jobs and for plowing ground at the large estates he was landscaping.

It was a time of prosperity and hard work. By the 1930s there were 60 employees and special expertise in azaleas, camellias, and the creation of rock gardens and fish ponds. Yoshimura was a leader in many community organizations and, as president of the Nurserymen's Association, arranged donation of plants to United States military bases in California.

But World War II abruptly intervened. The Yoshimuras and their children were sent to a relocation camp in Rivers, Arizona, with one son drafted and serving in the United States Army. The business and its valuable inventory would have to be sold.

At this critical point E. Manchester Boddy, publisher of the Los Angeles Daily News, came along. He had been buying plants at the Mission Nursery for his La Canada estate (now Descanso Gardens). He purchased the business at a fair price and operated it for the duration of the war.

When the Yoshimuras returned, they had the capital from this sale to begin anew. They settled on a nearby property, while Boddy closed the old nursery and took its plants to his estate. Visitors to Descanso Gardens today walk in a forest of large camellias, azaleas and rhododendrons, many of which came from the Mission Nursery.

To recreate stock for their new San Gabriel Nursery and Florist, the family planted fields of pansies where the present retail store is now. Customers of the 1940s bought the pansies not in flats as today, but by walking the fields and choosing the ones they wanted. The Yoshimuras also pitched tents at the nursery for other returning Japanese American families, until all were earning a living again.

In the next decades, seven new greenhouses were built, filled with poinsettias at Christmastime. The family created the bell-shaped flowering hybrid azalea named "Mission Bell." More than 60 agricultural trainees from Japan were welcomed at the nursery over the years.

Today the San Gabriel Nursery is still in the same family. Like a mature garden that has weathered the storms, it is mellow and full of life.

How to get there: The nursery is at 632 S. San Gabriel Blvd. From the 10 Freeway, exit at San Gabriel Blvd. and drive north. Call (626) 286-3782.

Smith Park

✧ *San Gabriel* ✧

IT'S LIVING HISTORY, it's pavement reverting to fresh green, and best of all, it's a chance to meet the original residents of our area: the Gabrielino-Tongva people. All this is at the playful village in San Gabriel's newly expanded Smith Park.

In 1996, the city purchased a parking lot just west of three-acre Smith Park. After removing the pavement and the intervening street, they were able to double the park size to nearly six acres. The existing park already held many activities: swimming and wading pools, basketball and tennis courts, playgrounds and lawns for sports. The new addition would have its own recreational and educational themes.

Landscape architects Armstrong and Walker cleared away the ugly asphalt and designed a gathering place to honor the tribal culture which flourished when the San Gabriel Mission was founded. Members of the Gabrieleno-Tongva Tribal Council worked closely on the project, bringing knowledge and the living spirit of their people.

Near this park once stood the Gabrielino-Tongva village of Sibangna, with a population of about 150 souls. It was mid-way

between the native villages of Kuukamongna and Yaangna (now Cucamonga and Los Angeles). More than 5,000 of these indigenous people lived in settlements dotting the valleys, foothills, and coastline of Los Angeles and  Orange Counties. Their relatives occupied the southern Channel Islands and traded back and forth across the sea.

The name Gabrielino was given to the native people as they were incorporated into the life of the Mission in the1700s and early 1800s. Today many of their descendants prefer to be known as the Tongva.

The new park is a tribute to their original life, close to the land. The park is ideal for picnics and unstructured play, with shade shelters resembling Tongva reed houses, and mounded lawns imitating ocean swells with concrete sea animals for climbing and imagining.

A dry stream bed and pond evoke those found in local foothills, while boulders and native trees create a niche of the natural landscape. Here are the plants used by the Tongva for their baskets, food, medicine, clothing and ceremonies. In the picnic area a huge concrete compass on the ground marks important directions of Tongva villages, trade routes and symbols.

The City of San Gabriel commissioned Dixie Giering, a local artist, to design a glorious tile mural, 4 by 18 feet, welcoming visitors to Smith Park. The hand painted mural shows scenes of Tongva life on one side, and richly detailed artifacts and symbols on the other. You could visit this mural many times and notice something new every time. It's a historic feast for the eye.

This nifty new park opened in July 2000 with a worthy celebration of tribal blessings, dance and music. There is a wealth of knowledge here on interpretive plaques, and a sniff of the sage will carry you to the native world. All ages will enjoy this unusual spot.

How to get there: Smith Park is at 232 West Broadway, just two blocks east of the San Gabriel Mission. For information and directions, call (626) 308-2875.

Huntington Desert Garden

✧ *San Marino* ✧

IF YOU LIKE old gardens, you may find them within modern ones when you know how to look. One of the oldest locally is the Desert Garden at the Huntington Botanical Gardens in San Marino.

Walking down the hill into the 12-acre garden, you'll see more than 5,000 species of plants and trees that have adapted to dry environments. Henry Huntington sat somewhere on that slope under a large sycamore tree about 1905, speaking with his estate superintendent William Hertrich. Huntington had bought the San Marino ranch several years before, and was eager to experiment with new plantings. But when Hertrich proposed a desert garden for that

spot, his employer claimed a strong dislike for all cacti.

Only by stressing scientific and educational value did Hertrich get permission for a modest start. Collecting trips to Southwestern states and Mexico followed.

Soon Huntington joined the "spirit of the chase," purchasing from other collectors and becoming proud of his new garden.

About 1925, the citrus orchards south of the Huntington

54

estate were subdivided for residential lots. Surplus soil was used to fill in a large open reservoir at the foot of the cactus garden. That provided the level four acres now forming the southern part of the garden.

To fill in the new area, many large specimen plants were transplanted, some weighing up to five tons. These giants, now 75 years later, are solidly established as the ancients of the garden. One craggy old Cereus xanthocarpus resembles elephant hide. A tall Yucca filifera has a trunk four feet in diameter.

Aloes, yuccas and the others bloom at various times, but this is mainly a garden of forms. What mind could have dreamed up such a crazy lot of shapes, thorns, spines and spires? It seems a mad designer has been at work creating these plants.

The boojum trees show a cock-eyed dignity, while the creeping devils (in the Baja California bed) snake their way close to the paths. The mammillaria are disguised as masses of pincushions. All these plants are survivors, being adapted to heat, winds and lack of water. Wooly coverings protect some from fierce sun. In others, like the golden barrel cactus, puffy shapes store moisture.

It's easy to sense personalities in these plants. The old patriarchs seem to preside calmly over the antics below. They may be marveling about how the younger generation is decking itself out. Some peppy adolescents seem to be chasing each other. The agaves are tailored in flowing green and gold fronds, while the little sedums cluster neatly. The whole scene is like a domestic comedy of the plant kingdom.

Birds and lizards dart safely among the spines. Even a squirrel can be seen high in an agave flower stalk, finding seeds 20 feet above ground. You can take all this in from a bench in the shade, or just saunter to catch the details of these strange life forms.

How to get there: The Huntington Library, Arts Collections, and Botanical Gardens is at 1151 Oxford Rd. From the 210 Freeway, exit at Allen Ave. and drive south into the Huntington's north gate. Call (626) 405-2100.

Los Robles (Stoneman Ranch)

✧ *San Marino* ✧

OF CALIFORNIA GOVERNOR George Stoneman's once spreading ranch, nothing remains now but a landmark plaque. But this quiet residential spot in San Marino was once called "the fruit belt of Los Angeles County."

Stoneman was born in New York state in 1822 and served in the Mexican War after finishing West Point with high honors. In 1853, he traveled to Fort Tejon in California with an Army railroad survey, and he met the Indian Agent for that region, Benjamin D. Wilson (Don Benito).

Wilson, later mayor of Los Angeles and twice a state senator, had reached California in 1841 and was establishing his Lake Vineyard Ranch beside present-day Lacy Park in San Marino. Fate would join the friends again in about two decades.

After the Civil War, General Stoneman left the Army and returned to California with his wife and four children. For $7,000, he bought 400 acres of choice land from Wilson in 1871 and became his neighbor.

He named the property "Los Robles" for its fine stand of oaks. His pastures, citrus groves, and vineyards were watered by Mill Spring Creek on the northeast border of the ranch.

Like his neighbor, Stoneman was a spirited political activist. He became a State Railway Commissioner in 1879 and was elected California's Governor by a wide margin in 1883. He and Wilson worked diligently for legislation benefitting agriculture.

Optimistically Stoneman once predicted the sale of 25,000 gallons of his wine and a market for all he could produce. He also distilled a smooth brandy called "zuny" made from cactus fruit.

The adventurous Stoneman tried in his furnaces the crude petroleum discovered in San Fernando in 1878. That year the Los Angeles Herald wrote: "It is quite possible even our orange, wine and brandy interests will be dwarfed in the next five years by our petroleum yield."

Guests at prosperous Los Robles included General John C. Fremont and, in 1880, U.S. President Rutherford B. Hayes.

When Daniel Berry of Indiana reached the area in the 1870s to establish a colony, he reported "Stoneman refuses $150 per acre for some of his unimproved land" (the Governor's cost had been just $17.50 per acre). Berry and the Indiana Colony later acquired 4,000 acres along the Arroyo Seco, which became the birthplace of Pasadena.

Stoneman's land fell in the prized "fruit belt," an area two miles wide by 10 miles long, defined by the journalist Ben Truman in his book "Semi-Tropical California" in 1874. This precious slope was protected by hills from ocean or canyon winds, and lifted above fogs which shrouded lowlands to the south. Truman often saw it standing out in clear sunshine, as though specially favored by nature.

The ranch buildings are gone now. But behind their historic marker still lies the land described as heavenly in climate and scenery, a theater for nature's most productive powers.

How to get there: The marker is at 1890 Montrobles Place in San Marino. From the 210 Freeway, exit at Lake Ave., drive south to Del Mar Ave., right to Los Robles Ave., left to Monterey Rd., and left to Montrobles Place (runs to left only).

Michael White Adobe

✧ *San Marino* ✧

VISITING A HISTORIC SITE, we try to look back along
that fourth dimension—time—and see the place as it once was.
Some spots in the Southland are so evocative that we can sense
their past. Other landmarks have lost their context, and we
must use our historical imaginations. So it is with the Michael
White Adobe.

This four-room structure is the oldest dwelling in San Marino. It
was built for a tiny rancho, granted to an Englishman by Pio Pico,
the last Mexican governor of California. Michael White held only
78 acres, set between the 14,000-acre San Pasqual ranch (later
Benjamin D. Wilson's) and the 13,300-acre Santa Anita ranch to the
east, the "Arcadia" of Lucky Baldwin.

White received his land grant, the San Ysidro Ranch, in 1845. His
early history is difficult to trace, although he told his life story which
was written down just before he died in 1885.

White shipped out from England on a whaling vessel at age 13. His ship's name, the "Perseverance," gave a fitting start for a life of adventures far from home, as he lived into his 80s. By his own account, he was stranded in Baja California, won an encounter with pirates, and later reached Santa Barbara. There he helped another adventurer, Joseph Chapman, build a schooner for travels to Mexico.

Reaching the San Gabriel Mission in 1830, White made a fortunate marriage to Maria del Rosario Guillen. His mother-in-law was Eulalia Perez de Guillen, who lived 100 years and was keeper of the keys at the Mission. Through her influence, Michael White was granted his ranch. He made a living there for his 13 children by growing grapes and doing carpentry work.

A stream ran near his house, and over yonder was the reedy Wilson Lake (now Lacy Park) in a natural hollow. The old Mission grist mill or El Molino Viejo, built in 1816 and a historic site today, was beside the lake. From the south White could hear the bells of the Mission.

The ranch passed through various owners until Henry Huntington founded the city of San Marino in 1913. The San Marino School District bought 18 acres of the property including the adobe in 1928 and leased them as a vegetable farm for years.

But the open lands are gone now, as the campus of San Marino High School was built in the 1950s right up to the old house. The adobe is currently occupied by the San Marino Historical Society to hold the city's historical papers and photos.

Today, squeezed between baseball fields and a swimming pool, the Michael White adobe appears stranded, without moorings to its past. But it has lived through 150 years of colorful Southland history. Just look up to the San Gabriel Mountains which are still its backdrop, and let your historical imagination do the rest.

How to get there: The adobe is completely enclosed by San Marino High School, 2701 Huntington Dr. From the 210 Freeway, exit at Sierra Madre Blvd. and drive south. Turn left on Huntington. To arrange a visit, ask at the San Marino Public Library (626) 300-0777.

Sts. Felicitas and Perpetua Church

⋄ *San Marino* ⋄

YES, IT'S A HANDSOME TOWER, and worthy to include in that sketchbook of Southland churches you may be starting. But there's much more in the surprising history of Sts. Felicitas and Perpetua Church in San Marino.

Church historian Mike Moran has ably researched 150 years and takes us back to an old adobe which stood on that spot. For the property now just west of Huntington Drive and San Gabriel Boulevard was once San Gabriel Mission land. In 1845, Governor Pio Pico granted about 70 acres here with a rough adobe house to the English sailor Michael White (known as Miguel Blanco).

White kept vineyards, then after 10 years moved to another adobe, half a mile to the west (now within the San Marino High School campus). In 1878, his lands were sold in foreclosure to Luther Harvey Titus, a rather fascinating New Yorker. Titus was a gentleman farmer and citrus grower who named his new spread the Dew Drop Ranch

or The Horseshoe, for the giant horseshoe spanning his entrance gate.

Titus added a second story to the adobe, with a wooden balcony all around. His groves prospered, and he invented the Titus Fumigator—a high, rolling contraption that was pushed along to dust for pests from above the trees. But his great love was horses, trotting horses.

In this matter he established a friendly rivalry with his neighbor to the east, Leonard J. Rose on the fabled Sunny Slope Ranch. Rose's son in his memoir "L.J. Rose of Sunny Slope" recalls that the two gentlemen's barns were just 500 feet apart, housing their famous breeding horses: Echo and The Moor (belonging to Titus and Rose respectively), which went on to sire champions.

When Titus sold the land, a later owner was L.L. Bradbury, whose foothill property is still known as Bradbury. His heirs lived in the adobe ranch house until the Bradbury Estate Co. subdivided the land into a development called Gainsborough Heath. They turned the old adobe into a romantically Spanish-styled restaurant, adding eight arches, a curving outdoor stairway and a tiled fountain. This oak-shaded spot was called La Ramada Inn (no relation to the Ramada Inn chain of today).

When the Depression ended this business, the adobe housed a tiny military school of about 20 boys for three years. Then the property became the site of Sts. Felicitas and Perpetua Church, built in 1948, and the historic adobe was its Rectory. In 1962, the adobe was demolished to build the present Rectory, ending the link to Mission days.

But step into the church now. Long, narrow and high, it is somehow very California-looking. The missions are in its pedigree somewhere. Saints windows glow in blue and ruby red. Contemporary small tapestries add to the minimal adornment. It's a tranquil space on a corner with a lively history.

How to get there: Sts. Felicitas and Perpetua Church is at 1190 Palomar Rd. From the 210 Freeway, exit at San Gabriel Blvd. and drive south; turn right on Huntington Dr. and right on Palomar. Call (626) 796-0432.

Essick House

✧ *Sierra Madre* ✧

IN 1972, by some good destiny, a civic organization losing its clubhouse met a classic California bungalow facing demolition. Thinking a violent windstorm was no bad omen, the members of the Sierra Madre Woman's Club chose the historic Essick House for their new home.

The Woman's Club is as old as the city. Records show that the men of Sierra Madre gathered in February 1907 to incorporate the town, and just three days later a group of women met to form a Woman's Club. 54 charter members set the club's educational, philanthropic (and originally "reformatory") goals.

Soon the club joined the General Federation of Women's Clubs, which would eventually have international membership of over 10 million women. In 1909, the club built a clubhouse where the town's civic center is today.

Cultural and educational activities started right away, as well as chicken pie dinners and strawberry fetes. The first Flower Festival in

the San Gabriel Valley, a three-day event, was held in 1911 with over 100 floral entries and a queen. In 1919, the club began to sponsor the annual Wistaria Fete, celebrating the famed vine planted in Sierra Madre in 1894 and now open to visitors one day every spring. Originally, these festivities lasted two or three weeks, attracting up to 100,000 visitors.

One Christmas the club's Santa Claus rode a burro down a canyon trail to bring gifts for the children. After Women's Suffrage was granted in the 1920s, the club took the lead with political forums. The clubhouse was often packed for community sings, art exhibits, melodramas, lectures and service projects.

But reluctantly the women sold their clubhouse to the city in 1969 and were temporarily bereft. Then they found the home designed and owned by one of their early members, Jennie Bryant Essick. She had lived there until 1935. The house was in sad disrepair and about to be lost. Could a community volunteer restoration effort save it?

The night before the club made its decision about the house, wild winds toppled an 80-foot deodar tree in the front yard, crushing the garden wall. Walking past this disaster, the members stepped into the Essick House and voted overwhelmingly that this would be their new home.

Franklin D. Howell III was the restoration architect, and over 50 organizations and businesses provided volunteer work. From ceilings to floors, the old house was renewed. The Sierra Madre Woman's Club again offered their home base for community meetings. Their educational and service activities continue now in a modern vein.

The Essick House, built around 1914, is a classic of Craftsman architecture. Its lines are strongly horizontal, its roofline nearly flat but stepped at three levels. Lattice work under the eaves and prominent rafter ends add interest. Typical of this style, the doorway is deeply sheltered within a porch. The front has an unusual curving bow window, and the house is clad in rich brown wood. It's a mellow spot for gatherings today.

How to get there: The Essick House is at 550 W. Sierra Madre Blvd. From the 210 Freeway, exit at Baldwin Ave. and drive north; turn left at Sierra Madre Blvd. Call (626) 355-4379.

Howard Whalen Sculpture Garden
✧ *Sierra Madre* ✧

ART AND NATURE mingle sociably in this unusual place, the Howard Whalen Sculpture Garden in Sierra Madre. It's just a sloping village lot, across a quiet street from the wild foothills, but some presiding spirit unifies the scene.

The garden was made by friends of the artist, Howard Whalen, to keep his memory alive and give a natural setting for his creations. Whalen was born in 1913 in Detroit and apprenticed at the Cranbrook Art Academy there. Later he taught sculpture at the University of Michigan School of Architecture. In World War II he served as infantryman and a G.I. cartoonist.

In California, he was also an actor and set designer, and always an observer of people. He supported himself as he could—sometimes acting in commercials or building models for tractor companies. He died in 1982.

His favorite sculpture technique was terra cotta, formed and fired directly, without casting in a mold. The rustic garden in Sierra Madre holds about 70 sculptures, of the 700-800 he did in his lifetime. You'll see the cartoonist coming out. It's amazing how these free forms can

suggest something alive: an animal? A head with feet? A horse sunbathing? Humor and mystery are in a dance here.

Whalen rarely gave his statues titles, so he wouldn't cramp the viewer's imagination. He wrote that his approach was "parallel to the fresh abstract feeling of jazz." Witness to this idea are three little jazz musicians captured in clay.

You might think of miniature Henry Moore figures, or Picasso. But Whalen had no such pretensions, according to his friends. He was just expressing the wit and life he saw in humanity, always experimenting and improvising. At the back of the garden his studio still holds shelves of small figures, along with the art works of friends.

The garden was designed by Larry Dolan. Gravelly paths meander or disappear; it doesn't matter which. Boulders have casually dropped by, forming little terraces. The sound of water comes from a terra cotta fountain, and you'll hear mourning doves, maybe woodpeckers.

Assorted cactus and aloe plants have the same quirky quality as the figures. Momentary seriousness comes from a healthy oak and old citrus trees left over from a grove. Bamboo and sycamore add to the appealing jumble.

Volunteers are always welcome to help tend the garden, affirming the power of an individual artist to have his say and to remain with us. This is a satisfying thought.

In this sunny spot, all is rustic, a bit haphazard, and yet unified. It's a little world. . . the world of Howard Whalen's art.

How to get there: The garden is at 62 E. Carter St. From the 210 Freeway exit at Baldwin Ave. and drive north to the top; turn right on Carter. Contact the Sculpture Garden at P.O. Box 311, Sierra Madre, CA 91025. The Garden has traditionally been open on Saturdays, 10 – 12 a.m.

Old North Church

✧ *Sierra Madre* ✧

THE SIGN READS "Old North Church" on the white-steepled church in Sierra Madre, calling up mistaken echoes of Paul Revere. But this is no fragment of New England, planted at the foot of California chaparral slopes. There's a more practical reason for its name.

The church dates almost from the founding of the town. Nathaniel C. Carter of Lowell, Mass., had come to California in 1871 for his health. In 1881 he bought land from "Lucky" Baldwin, the Southern Pacific Railroad, and John Richardson, combining 1,103 acres to start the town of Sierra Madre.

Carter laid out his community in 20 and 40-acre lots. Roads ran off to surrounding villages, with Los Angeles six or seven hours ride away and all uphill returning home. By 1883 there were 17 families, from New England, the Midwest, the British Isles. The land boom of 1886-87 touched the little foothill town, and soon the tracts were subdivided.

About that time, the town's Anglicans formed the Church of the Ascension. Their

1888 stone church in Sierra Madre is now on the National Register of Historic Places.

Thirteen other believers from various Protestant denominations joined in a Union Church. They met first in the former school house of the Baldwin Ranch, then in the town hall, then the public library.

At last in 1890, they completed their own new church, modeled after a church in Holland. The tower was added in 1893 and originally had no steeple but a simple cap-roof, looking far more Dutch than it does today. The San Gabriel Mountains showed through the tall narrow openings in the tower. Later the church was painted white.

Kept since the early days are the records of the church's Ladies Social Union, later called the Ladies Aid Society. The story of their doings, 1888 – 1950, is a social history of a small Southern California town—a dynamic and lovable group of women, their strength, humor and energy shining out.

After the ladies raised "a goodly sum" for the new church, "they loaned their money to the local water company at a good rate of interest." More funds flowed in from baked-bean suppers, ice cream socials, and concerts in costume.

Over the years, young and old joined them for spelling bees, quilting, literary readings and sewing for war relief in World War I. The foods, pastimes, and civic concerns of three generations can all be seen. Every 100-year-old church should have such a record of its joys and cares together.

In 1928, the growing Sierra Madre Congregational Church moved into its new building just across the boulevard. The large new stone church and meeting halls were designed in a Renaissance style by Howard Morgridge.

Today the original clapboard church is still used by the congregation for classes and meetings. Just north of the "new" sanctuary, it is now fittingly called the Old North Church.

How to get there: The Old North Church is at 191 Sierra Madre Blvd. From the 210 Freeway, exit at Baldwin Ave., drive north, turn left at Sierra Madre Blvd. Call (626) 355-3566.

Cawston Ostrich Farm

✧ *South Pasadena* ✧

SEVERAL YEARS AGO, in 1996, South Pasadena proclaimed the Centennial Year of the Ostrich in its town. Why this homage to the giant bird?

In 1896, an Englishman named Edwin Cawston moved his growing business from Norwalk to a 12-acre site in South Pasadena. Cawston's Ostrich Farm was then well on its way to fame and fashion.

Ostrich feathers had been used in costumes since the Middle Ages, and in 1896 they were the rage for ladies' capes, boas and hats. Cawston had traveled to South Africa in 1885, bent on purchasing a troop (not to be called a flock) of the 8-foot tall birds. Of the 52 he imported by ship to Texas, then by rail to California, just a few survived. But with their fertile eggs, he soon had a population of 260.

By one account, Cawston's feathered charges finally numbered about 3,000 in South Pasadena. He had several thousand more on his 400-acre breeding farm in San Jacinto. Cawston was a master

salesman who made his semi-tropical ostrich park a tourist showplace. His grounds included an incubator house, dye house, factory building for feathered creations, and a salesroom. The Pacific Electric rail line passed the front gate, then carried visitors onward to the San Gabriel Mission and Gay's Lion Farm in El Monte.

The male birds' wing and tail feathers were the most prized, and the birds could be plucked several times a year. The ostriches could live as long as 80 years and weighed up to 300 pounds. Some were trained to carry a human rider or to pull visitors in two wheeled carts.

Farm guests were enthralled by the mammoth creatures, their huge eggs, and the chicks (as big as chickens when hatched and growing a foot a month). In 1900, Cawston's plumes won a gold medal at the World's Exposition in Paris. The enterprising Englishman even tried out early forms of solar power at his farm.

In 1909, South Pasadena citizens considered renaming their town (to correct the misconception that it was part of Pasadena), but Cawston argued that the town's good name was already known worldwide, through his advertising.

As fashions changed, Cawston shrewdly sold his operation in 1911 and returned to his native Cobham, England. The business carried on until 1935, then closed. It was remembered as the most successful and long-lasting of the ostrich farms that had once thrived in Africa, Europe and America.

Gradually the farm's buildings disappeared, including Cawston's 22-room house. In the 1980s the last structure was demolished, making way for light industry on the site.

Today only a historic marker shows the place once hailed as "the original, the pioneer, the greatest and largest of all its kind—one of the institutions of Southern California." And this explains why a lifesize stuffed-animal ostrich benignly watches visitors entering the South Pasadena Public Library.

How to get there: The marker is at 100 Pasadena Ave., South Pasadena. From the 210 Freeway, exit at Fair Oaks Ave., drive south to Mission St., turn right, then veer left at Pasadena Ave. For information call the South Pasadena Preservation Foundation at (626) 799-9089.

Holy Family Church
✧ *South Pasadena* ✧

AN EARLY PHOTOGRAPH shows a snug brown shingle cottage with a stone chimney, a typical dwelling in small town South Pasadena about 1910. But why that cross atop the roof? This was the first home of the fledgling Holy Family Church.

Soon the cottage was replaced by a new "bungalow church" on the corner now occupied by the city's Post Office at Fremont and El Centro. Several large Southland churches first went through these simple stages resembling little wooden houses.

Then the Roman Catholic congregation set about raising money for a more sizable church in a flurry of bazaars, picnics and card parties. The result was the present Holy Family Church, a Spanish Baroque landmark dedicated in 1928 with more than 100 priests at the festive ceremony. The architect was Emmett G. Martin and the builder Charles W. Pettifer and Co.

The building is a substantial presence, with its golden hue and a bell tower rising to 90 feet. Carved stone ornamentation surrounds the entrance portals and the windows of the north and south transepts. The façade holds bronze statues of the Holy Family and two bas-relief stone medallions showing Christ's boyhood.

Details of the tower pierced with windows and decked out with carved stone borders are well worth studying. A Moorish tile dome adds dash and color.

Inside, the architect specified mahogany pews and open trusses of redwood to support the roof. Later additions included carved mahogany side altars, stained glass windows from France, and carillon chimes added in the Bicentennial Year of 1976.

The life of this parish always involved education, as the Holy Family School was established in 1927. The Sisters of Loretto were the original teachers, and various buildings have been created for the school over the years. Today these surround the church and share its honey-colored hue.

High points of the congregation's history include the Annual Fall Festival, sometimes held at the South Pasadena Woman's Clubhouse across the street. In the 1930s, this event featured such film celebrities as Joan Crawford and Spencer Tracy.

For the church's 75th Jubilee Year, in 1985, the members planted 75 trees in South Pasadena and 75 rose bushes in the city's Garfield Park.

Martin's exuberant design invites comparison with another Roman Catholic church of the 1920s, the serenely white St. Elizabeth's Church in Altadena, designed by Wallace Neff and completed in 1926.

Both are fine subjects for camera or sketchbook. Martin's church fills your eyes with detail, while Neff makes beautiful composition out of simple forms and arches. In fact, a visit to Holy Family Church might be the start of your own sketch portfolio of church towers, which are so varied in our entertaining Southland architecture. See what you can find.

How to get there: Holy Family Church is at 1501 Fremont Ave. From the 110 Freeway, exit at Fair Oaks Ave. and drive south. Turn right on Mission St. and left on Fremont. Call (626) 799-8908.

Mission West District

✧ *South Pasadena* ✧

THERE IS SAFETY in numbers. You know this is true for people –
but it can also hold true for buildings.

Consider, for example, a thriving young city, incorporated in
1888 with its business district along a street called Mission. Soon
the wood and brick commercial structures were the heart of South
Pasadena.

With decades of growth, the coming and going of various railroads,
and pressure for change, what would happen to the oldest buildings
there? They might have been lost, one at a time. The solution was to
create a historic business district called Mission West, now listed on
the National Register of Historic Places, that would protect them all
together.

The district extends along Mission from Fairview to Meridian
Streets and is mapped in an illustrated leaflet called "South
Pasadena History & Landmarks." The leaflet is a treasury of
historic walks.

The buildings of this special area date from 1906 to 1924 and are all in use today. One is the former Mission Arroyo Hotel, built in 1923. It originally held lodgings on the second floor and shops at ground level. "New, modern, all outside rooms. Near streetcars and restaurants," said an early advertisement. The rates were $6 to $7 per week.

Today the brick building, recently restored, holds stores below and four apartments above. It used to face the city's old train depot (now gone), but history repeats itself, and it will soon be facing a stop on the new Gold Line of light rail from Los Angeles.

Other buildings protected in the Mission West district include the Meridian Iron Works (1887), which has been a general store, a school, an iron foundry, and more. It now holds the South Pasadena Historical Museum. Also included is the South Pasadena Bank building, a brick commercial structure with doorway recessed in cut-away arches. Opposite the former bank is the South Pasadena Public Library, a Carnegie library built in 1907 and since enlarged.

Just across from the Iron Works is the stone watering trough and wayside stop, created in 1906 as a resting place for people and horses traveling between Pasadena and Los Angeles. Back at the Mission Arroyo Hotel, you'll find across the street to the east the "Century House" (1888), a Midwestern style frame house with Eastlake gables – given its name in 1988 at the city's centennial.

All these are part of the historic district, as are several other vintage brick buildings along Mission Street. The focus of the area is now arts and antiques, with farmers' markets and some lively festivals. You might hear a blue grass fiddle for dancing in the streets.

How to get there: Pick up the map leaflet at the Historical Museum (Meridian Iron Works), 913 Meridian Ave. From the 110 Freeway, exit at Fair Oaks Ave. and drive south. Turn right on Mission St., then left on Meridian. For hours, call (626) 799-9089.

Raymond Hill
✧ *South Pasadena* ✧

A HILLTOP is a fine vantage point on a clear winter day, when you have views in all directions. Visiting the top of Raymond Hill in South Pasadena, you'll be at a meeting point of geography and history.

Raymond Hill (originally called Bacon Hill) is one of the highest elevations in the western San Gabriel Valley, at the southern border of Pasadena just east of Fair Oaks Avenue. Walter Raymond of the Boston-based tour agency Raymond and Whitcomb was attracted here in 1883, seeking a hotel site for his clients. He was just 31 years of age.

Acquiring 55 acres of the stunning hilltop, Raymond set out to remove 34 feet of its height to make a flat area for his hotel. The prodigious job took four months as 250 men drilled and blasted away at the granite monolith. The crown of the hill eventually held two hotels, one from 1886-1895 and the second from 1901-1934.

The first Raymond Hotel opened in glory and a downpour, with some 1,500 guests for the festivities. The Royal Raymond (it was later called) had four stories, 201 rooms and 40 bathrooms, and a French-looking silhouette with three towers.

Best of all were its views. Catalina Island was visible from the south-facing veranda. The foothills beyond South Pasadena hid the growing town of Los Angeles, leaving a rural landscape all around. To the north the San Gabriel Mountains made a picturesque wall, and to the east was the snowclad San Bernardino range.

The original Raymond was destroyed by fire on Easter Sunday 1895. But the heyday of mid-winter visitors was still at hand. So in 1901, Walter Raymond's son Arthur, age 2, pulled open the ribbons of a new and larger Raymond Hotel—Moorish in style with 275 guest rooms and 110 bathrooms. Its towers, turrets and columns could be seen for miles perched high on the hill. Just to the south spread a new 20-acre pleasure ground with a golf course, tennis and croquet.

Andrew Carnegie, Theodore Roosevelt and many others stayed to enjoy the famous panorama. But changing tastes and economic hard times brought a final sunset to the second Raymond. It was razed in 1934, the same year Walter Raymond died.

Today Raymond Hill is covered with modest apartment dwellings and mature trees. As you stroll its curving roads, you'll definitely feel above the fray—but you'll have to look between buildings to piece together the famous views. Mount Baldy lifts its snowy crest in winter, while Mount Wilson (north) and Mount Lukens (farther west) are spiky with communication towers. Looking toward downtown Los Angeles, you can see just the top of the tallest skyscraper (73 stories) rising above the Monterey Hills.

Along the southern edge of the hilltop a low old stone wall curves above a retaining wall. Here, imagine a carriage coming up the hill, bringing Eastern guests to Walter Raymond's grand hotel just behind you.

How to get there: From the 210 Freeway, exit at Fair Oaks Ave. Drive south; turn left on Raymond Hill Rd. For information, call the South Pasadena Preservation Foundation (626) 799-9089.

South Pasadena Woman's Club

✧ *South Pasadena* ✧

IT'S BEEN A BUSY 101 YEARS for the South Pasadena Woman's Club. And the members got busy right away, seeing work that needed to be done in their fledgling town of 500 people in 1899.

That year, a group of spirited women met at the home of Mrs. Leo Longley to form the Women's Improvement Association (the club's original name). Immediately they took on a local eyesore: the rubbishy area around the town's Santa Fe Railroad depot. Leasing the land from the railroad for $1 a year, they cleared the rubble and planted a small park as a worthy entrance to South Pasadena. The old depot is gone now, but the little park will soon greet travelers at the city's stop on the light railway, the Gold Line.

In 1907 the club gave the massive stone watering trough still in front of the Meridian Iron Works (that's the city's historical museum, just south of Mission Street on Meridian Avenue). The water station

76

was marked: "for the comfort of Man and Beast," offered for travelers and riders on their way to Los Angeles.

The purpose of this energetic club was to improve South Pasadena and to hold informative programs. The club had four study sections: literature, social and civic questions, art, and education. Members often responded to roll call with a quotation on a subject previously assigned.

Their interest in parks continued, and some of the city's mature trees owe their lives to the Women's Improvement Association, which protected trees from unnecessary cutting. In 1911 the club also helped to establish a park in the Arroyo Seco.

The club was a bit nomadic in its early years, meeting at members' homes, the Baptist Church, the city council chambers, a hotel parlor, and a local school. Then, under a beautiful June sky in 1913, they laid the cornerstone for their own clubhouse at the corner of Fremont Avenue and Rollin Street. The architect was Norman Foote Marsh, designer of many homes and public buildings in the area, including parts of South Pasadena High School.

The brown shingle building is a solid presence today on its corner, across from the Holy Family Church. Marsh created interesting rooflines and a spacious interior, with parlors, meeting rooms, and an auditorium the whole community has enjoyed.

In 1924, when Mrs. Norman Marsh was president of the club, its name was changed to the Woman's Club of South Pasadena. It belongs to the General Federation of Women's Clubs, a nationwide alliance which has been important in our country's history.

With projects in wartime and philanthropy in peacetime, the club has carried on its work and its studies. Today, it presents scholarships to local high school students and handmade items to hospitals and children.

And you too can share in their versatile home, for the members welcome use of their historic clubhouse for weddings, parties, and special events.

How to get there: To reach 1424 Fremont Ave., from the 110 Freeway exit at Fair Oaks Ave. and drive south. Turn right on Mission St. and left on Fremont. Call (626) 799-9309.

Pico Rivera Museum

Baldwin Park Historical Museum
✧ *Baldwin Park* ✧

MUSEUMS SOMETIMES must move from place to place, carrying their best-loved belongings with them just as a family would. The Baldwin Park Historical Museum now invites history-minded visitors to this little building in the heart of town.

Pleasant View was the first name for a village on this site (about 1878), changed to Vineland in 1887. A public school and Vineland Irrigation District anchored the growing settlement in the 1890s. All around it towns were springing up on the old ranchos: Ranchos Azusa Duarte and Azusa Dalton on the north, Ranchos San Jose and La Puente on the east, more of Rancho La Puente to the south, and Rancho San Francisquito to the west.

Promoters here described the rich river-plain soil as abundantly growing "all kinds of garden vegetables, berries, carnations, violets, oranges and walnuts."

Elias Jackson "Lucky" Baldwin had become owner of Rancho La Puente, and he intended to subdivide parts of his large land holdings. In 1906 residents of Vineland heard that Baldwin might be planning a large new town, Baldwinville, just south of them. To deter this rival, the Vinelanders proudly invited Baldwin to visit them and

support their community with his name. He consented, and so Baldwin Park was named.

That same year, the Pacific Electric Railroad line was extended along Ramona Boulevard, the central axis of the town, and the Chamber of Commerce was organized. The new Baldwin Park Woman's Club became a source of civic strength like so many women's clubs in the Southland.

The museum shows records of the town's growth. You'll see a 1944 map of the area which calls Baldwin Park "the Gateway to the Orange Empire, and Hub of the San Gabriel Valley." Located 17 miles east of Los Angeles, the town held poultry ranches, walnut and citrus groves, manufacturing concerns and sand/gravel companies. The Santa Fe Dam, then the world's largest earth-filled dam, had been built just to the north in the early 1940s. Baldwin Park incorporated in 1956, when some dairies and chicken ranches still existed, then grew in the postwar years.

Like many small museums of the San Gabriel Valley, this one is something of a kaleidoscope. You'll find just little pieces on each historical subject, but altogether the bits make patterns.

A display of women's clothing is casually arranged, showing the sartorial revolution that took place between 1900 and 1925. Military uniforms, including a World War II WAC outfit, make another theme.

Early machinery shows the time-consuming effort once needed for daily work. A washing machine from the 1930s, underwear hanging next to a wood- or coal-burning stove, an intricate loom, all reveal domestic life.

Other vocations shown are an early school room, the citrus industry and a blacksmith's shop. The museum holds a great collection of four-foot-long panorama photographs, old books, pamphlets and newspapers all recording the history of the little town Lucky Baldwin liked.

How to get there: The Museum is at 4061 Sterling Way. From the 605 Freeway, exit at Ramona Blvd. and drive east. Turn right on Baldwin Park Blvd. and immediately left on Sterling. Call (626) 338-7130.

Bodger Seeds Ltd.

⬦ *South El Monte* ⬦

WHERE DO NEW flower varieties come from?

Bodger Seeds Ltd., a pioneer El Monte firm, has been answering that question for about 100 years. The company was established by John Bodger, who came to California from England in 1890, and now it is one of the world's largest wholesale flower seed producers.

First the Bodger family created in Gardena a large sweet pea farm which tourists visited via Pacific Electric Red Cars from Los Angeles, 12 miles away. Then in 1916 they began to purchase land in El Monte. Early settlers had called the area "El Monte" or "the wooded place" because of its abundant willow thickets along the San Gabriel River.

For 50 years, walnut groves covered much of the land. But finally production dwindled and pests threatened the old trees. The Bodgers saw an ideal micro-climate for certain flowers: clear, dry air, good tempera-ture range and a soil of rich loam. By 1924 they had cleared their lands and planted 150 acres of zinnias and 150 of asters. They also contracted with other owners to grow seed for them, making a total ranch of 1,200 blooming acres.

Gradually the El Monte land was sold and the growing shifted to Lompoc in Northern California. There, during World War II, the company grew the famous floral American flag composed of red, white and blue larkspur. It covered 12 acres and was a magnet to visitors as the old sweet pea farm had been.

In 1935 the firm donated a block of its land to El Monte for a new civic center, including the library (now the historical museum) and government buildings. Later they sold to the city the fields just across the street for a park.

Now the company distributes seeds to some 50 countries around the world. Heading the firm are third and fourth generation family members.

And where have the Bodgers' new flower varieties come from? One source has been "sports of nature" or freaks. In 1914 John Bodger spotted an off-type flower in a zinnia field, and watched it closely. "The mule pulling the cultivator stepped on it once, but it survived," recalls Bodger's granddaughter Louise Bodger Whitman. Carefully propagated, the new plant was marketed as 'Dahlia-Flowered' Zinnia and won a Gold Medal from Britain's Royal Horticultural Society.

Today the South El Monte offices display 153 awards for new varieties introduced by Bodger Seeds. These include the first red petunia ('Firechief'), nasturtium 'Golden Gleam', and hybrid marigolds with names like 'Gold Coins', 'Galores', 'Moonshot', and 'Apollo.'

The walnut groves and the flower fields are gone now, but many of El Monte's favorable growing conditions still exist, benefiting home gardeners there. When you visit the El Monte Historical Museum or the Tony Arceo Memorial Park across Tyler Avenue, you are on land where the Bodgers once grew a sea of cosmos and zinnias.

For more information: Visit the El Monte Historical Museum, 3100 Tyler Ave., El Monte. Call (626) 444-3813. From the 605 Freeway, exit at the 10 Freeway and drive west. Exit on Peck Rd; drive south. Turn right on Garvey Ave. and right on Tyler.

Gay's Lion Farm
✧ *El Monte* ✧

SEVENTY YEARS AGO the residents of El Monte, then a small town, had a strange local chorus. Citizens grew accustomed to a concert of fierce roars that peaked on Monday nights. The source? Two hundred lions at Gay's Lion Farm.

Visiting the Southwest and not seeing Gay's Lion Farm would be like visiting Egypt and not seeing the pyramids – so said advertising leaflets sent throughout the country in the 1920s and 30s. The farm operated for twenty years on five acres of land, at the crossroads of Valley Boulevard and Peck Road in El Monte. Today, despite efforts of history-minded citizens, the site has disappeared under the San Bernardino (10) Freeway.

Charles Gay, a Frenchman, visited a zoo outside Paris on his 10th birthday. There he touched a lion cub and wished to have one of his own some day. Later he began training animals in England and eventually brought a shipment of elephants, tigers and lions to Hollywood for use in silent films.

He and his wife soon bought lions of their own and purchased their El Monte property in 1922. The climate reminded the

Gays of Kenya, where they had traveled. In 1925 they opened their farm to the public with 57 lions. The grounds, with lion house, sunny yards, and arena for performances, were entered right through the Gays' home.

Everyone came. Hundreds of visitors each year admired the fiercest lions, Cyclone, Mars and Dynamite. More trainable were Aladdin, Nero, Duke and Leo—Duke starred in many movies, and Leo is the majestic lion roaring in the Metro-Goldwyn-Mayer logo that opened MGM films. These kingly beasts and many more were born at Gay's Lion Farm.

Photographs now in the El Monte Historical Museum show such visitors as Mae West and Eleanor Roosevelt, who came in 1933 with her son Elliott.

"Lions are extremely difficult to tame," wrote Charles Gay, "and are never reliable." Danger was always at hand, as lions never lose their savage nature. Each adult lion has 18 claws (five on each front paw and four on each hind one). They may stand seven feet tall and weigh up to 500 pounds. Gay and the trainers bore the scars of claws despite their patient handling of their charges.

And why the special roaring on Mondays? The lions were not fed that day, to rest their stomachs, as lions in the wild will gorge themselves and then go without food for a time.

Because of World War II shortages, the farm closed in 1942 and the 277 resident lions were sent to zoos and preserves. In 1949-50, Clyde Beatty leased the Lion Farm to film some jungle pictures. Then all was quiet and finally the freeway covered the property.

Now the plaster lions once in front of Gay's Lion Farm stand as mascots at the entrance to El Monte High School. And pictures abound at the excellent El Monte Historical Museum, just a block away.

How to get there: The Historical Museum is at 3150 N. Tyler Ave. From the 605 Freeway, turn west on the 10 Freeway. Exit on Peck Rd., go south to Garvey Ave., then right to Tyler Ave. and turn right. Call (626) 444-3813.

Santa Fe Dam

◇ *Irwindale* ◇

WHAT A WIDE LEGACY is left by a sweeping event of nature. In March 1938, rain fell steadily for several days here, turning Southern California into a watery landscape. These famous floods changed our geography and our coexistence with the wild streams.

But as the Southland population was growing, a truce had to be made with rivers like the San Gabriel River, which had ranged freely across its broad flood plain for centuries. One result was the four-mile wide Santa Fe Dam, which now holds a county park in its 1,188-acre reservoir area.

The upper San Gabriel Canyon already had several dams in 1938, but these were topped by the great flood. So in 1941, ground was broken for the new dam with more than 3,000 people attending the ceremonies.

This is an earthen dam, its core made of decomposed granite which is almost as hard as cement when wet. Tons of large rocks cover the U-shaped dam, 92 feet in height. It was built

by four construction companies and the U.S. Army Corps of Engineers.

Lack of material and manpower slowed the project during World War II, but the dam was completed in 1949. Today the dam covers 34,800 acres and its drainage area is 236 square miles. The flood control basin stretches from the 210 Freeway to Arrow Highway, and from the 605 Freeway to Irwindale Avenue.

Behind the dam, the City of Azusa wanted to put a public air field, but this was turned down because of the risk of floods. (Before World War II, many little landing fields had dotted the San Gabriel Valley).

Public use was established when Los Angeles County opened the Santa Fe Dam Recreational Area in 1974. This diverse park has 830 acres developed for swimming, fishing, camping, hiking and picnicking. The southern shore of the lake has a sandy beach, and small boats may use the waters (but no power boats). Trout and catfish are stocked for fishing, and there are miles of paved bicycling trails away from cars.

Stone picnic shelters and shady lawns are fun for groups. The park headquarters is in a stone building just east of the lake, offering information. An adult walking club enjoys the miles of paths on weekdays.

North of the lake is a nature trail, a pleasant loop starting from a currently closed nature center building. Bring your own field guide to native plants, and you'll find blooms much of the year.

Early morning or late afternoon (park hours are now 6:30 a.m. to 8 p.m.) are best for the nature trail, as that area is a suncatcher of colossal scale by day. And this is bird heaven, with its blend of coastal sage scrub and chaparral plant communities. You can roam to your heart's delight, in all seasons of the year, spotting birds of the lake, the brisk little goldfinches, and the desert-loving cactus wrens.

Be sure to call ahead, to see what activities are open when you plan to go.

How to get there: From the 210 Freeway, exit at Irwindale Ave. and drive south, turn right on Arrow Highway and immediately right on the dam entrance road. Call (626) 334-1065.

Neff Park

✧ *La Mirada* ✧

THIS MUST BE ONE of the prettiest spots you could find for a sunny day picnic, with 10 acres of hilly lawns, mature trees and three historic buildings that suggest a mini-estate. And it isn't far from home, at Neff Park in the heart of busy La Mirada.

As you open your picnic basket think about the 500 acres of olives and 300 acres of citrus (mostly lemons) that once surrounded this place, when it was headquarters of the Windermere Ranch, established by Andrew McNally in 1888. In Chicago, his Rand-McNally Co. was prosperous, making maps and guidebooks in the heyday of the railroads.

Then, attracted by the balmy winters of Southern California, McNally came west, bought 2,300 acres of rough sheep-grazing land known as Rancho Los Coyotes, and developed it with irrigation and groves. He planned to divide some of the ranch into 20-acre parcels as Country Gentlemen's Estates, but after the depression of the 1890s few were sold and that idea was abandoned.

At Windermere in 1893, McNally built a large home for his daughter Nannie and her husband Edwin Neff. There the second of their six children was born, the well-loved Southern California architect Wallace Neff.

In the meantime, Andrew McNally lived in his beautiful Queen Anne-style home in Altadena (still there, as a private residence), often checking on Windermere and those lively grandchildren.

With its modern processing plant, the ranch became famous for its olive oil shipped from the Santa Fe depot on the property. Southern California's resort hotels, like the Green in Pasadena and the Raymond in South Pasadena, bought many cases of McNally's Olive Oil, and the Jergens Co. used it in facial creams.

Around their home, the Neff family planted more than 100 ornamental trees from around the world. Many of those trees, now a century old, are still standing and are marked with their names.

The boyhood home of Wallace Neff was innovative for 1893. Its style is Mission Revival, made of stucco with a tile roof. The architect was Frederick Roehrig, who also designed Pasadena's Hotel Green. Wallace Neff became known for his own California style, using touches of England, France and Spain in his house designs.

The Windermere Ranch was managed by the Robert McGill family, then by Bill Neff (brother of Wallace) from 1940-62. In 1962 Bill Neff sold most of the land to developers who were creating the city of La Mirada (McNally's original name for his Land Co.). The railroad station, so long an agricultural hub, could not be kept, but remembering the famed groves each new homesite was to have an olive tree.

Today Neff Park contains the family home, a barn filled with mementos, and the George House, a picturesque Victorian used by the ranch overseer and now by a park caretaker. Where generations of Neff children frolicked, you too can picnic, enjoying this slice of history in the welcoming shade.

How to get there: Neff Park is at 14300 San Cristobal in La Mirada. From the Santa Ana (5) Freeway, exit at Rosecrans Ave. and drive east. Turn right on Biola Ave. and right on San Cristobal. The historic buildings are open several days each month; call (562) 943-7277 for information about open dates.

La Puente
Heritage Room and Archives
◇ *La Puente* ◇

MOST COMMUNITIES of the San Gabriel Valley have some repository holding the town's old photographs and maps. An afternoon in one of these places will lead you to more historical discoveries.

In La Puente, the spot for such research would be the La Puente Heritage Room and Archives, located in the City Hall on Main Street. When you find a settlement along a Main Street, crossed by First, Second and Third streets, you can guess it is the old heart of a town. Here you are in the township of Puente, which was laid out in 1886.

The Rowland-Workman Party first reached this land in 1841. Two friends, William Workman and John Rowland, led a party of some 30 settlers. They traveled the Santa Fe Trail from New Mexico and were the first overland immigrants to arrive in Southern California. They drove a flock of sheep with them and reported few hardships on the journey.

Rowland and Workman located a spacious valley, edged with low hills, where a spring-fed creek flowed westward to the San Gabriel

River. In 1842 they were granted 48,790 acres of this land—the Rancho La Puente once belonging to the San Gabriel Mission. Workman lived on the south bank of the San Jose Creek, and Rowland on the north bank. Homes of both these pioneers are still standing, in the City of Industry. (Workman's is part of the Workman and Temple Homestead Museum. Rowland's, pictured here, is awaiting restoration.)

In 1886, John Rowland's son sold part of the land to the firm of Pomeroy and Stimson, for a townsite. Typically a hotel came first, and so the Rowland Hotel was built that same year, a four-square design with round tower and wide veranda.

Other buildings soon clustered around. The compact village included the Stimson Building (a two-story general store, its upper floor used as dance hall and Protestant meeting place), a Southern Pacific Depot, and a small Catholic church.

Just to the east, the vineyards of Casimir Didier climbed the hillside. Didier was one of three brothers born in France who came to La Puente to raise sheep and dairy cows. Irrigation ditches as long as six miles brought water from the life-giving creek for the vines, alfalfa and pastures. In 1906 Casimir started a winery just steps away from the Rowland Hotel.

These buildings are gone now, and today Main Street in La Puente holds a small 1920s and 30s commercial district. But the architecture and life of generations before is very evident in the archives, in their photographs, maps, and mementos. Once you have explored the old pictures, you will be able to imagine the pioneering settlement, embraced by friendly hills.

Where are the historical archives of your own town? To find out, call your public library or chamber of commerce for more information.

How to get there: The La Puente Heritage Room and Archives is at 15900 E. Main St. From the 60 Freeway, exit at Hacienda Blvd. and drive north, turn right at Glendora Ave. and left on Main. For hours, call (626) 855-7000

Montebello Woman's Club
✧ *Montebello* ✧

HISTORY LOVERS, here is some inspiration for you. The story begins in April 1909, when 17 women gathered in a little town east of Los Angeles, on the San Gabriel River. Their homes in Montebello were scattered, and the city seemed far away. Banding together, they formed the Montebello Woman's Club, with dues of 25 cents a year.

Montebello incorporated as a city in 1920, and five years later the women opened their new clubhouse. It was in Spanish Colonial Revival style, built at a cost of $17,000. A handsome arched colonnade ran along the north side. The sitting room had a Mayan-accented fireplace, and beyond was a meeting hall with kitchen.

Keeping up its history of community service, the club founded and staffed the first library in Montebello, sold World War I bonds and stamps, and assisted the Red Cross in both world wars. The club hosted the Southern California Baseball Association annual meeting in 1927, and held Montebello High School junior proms from the 1930s through the 1950s. All this and more took place in the spacious building.

Present club members recall when the hills of Montebello were covered with nurseries (after all, the city's name means "beautiful mountain.") The State Flower Shows were held in the woman's clubhouse for many years, coordinated by the members. A joyful event in March 1944 was the mortgage-burning dinner.

The years passed, occupied with well-baby clinics, scouts and community meetings, and ceremonies to award academic and music scholarships to high school students. Any building would look worn after so much activity. Structural weakening began to need major attention.

At that point, current Club president Mary Metz was determined to affirm the historical significance of the building and to see it restored. With many months of work, passing first the city, then the county, state, and national levels of review, the women reached their goal: the clubhouse was listed on the National Register of Historic Places in 1995.

With the National Register listing came the opportunity to apply for funds, and now the building has been renewed both inside and out. Historical documents and paintings by members hang on view. The club is fortunate, for the broad greens of Montebello Park are just across the street.

California's club women have long been vital to community strength. The National Register recognizes this importance to social history as well as the architectural grace of the building.

The Montebello Woman's Club joined the General Federation of Women's Clubs in 1913 and continues its life within that network. Today, it will also arrange for other organizations to hold events at its clubhouse. The Club's motto helps to explain its longevity: "In essentials, unity; in non-essentials, liberty; in all things, charity." To these ideals, the women of Montebello added determination – and they saved their historic building.

How to get there: The Montebello Woman's Club is at 201 S. Park Ave. From the 605 Freeway, exit at Whittier Blvd. and drive west. Turn left at Park Ave. Call (323) 725-8002.

Hargitt House

✧ *Norwalk* ✧

NO MATTER how many heritage houses you visit around the Southland, each one is as distinct as an individual face. Consider, for example, the Hargitt House in Norwalk, south of Whittier. This two-story Victorian farmhouse, built in 1891, is in the Eastlake style. It has tall narrow windows reaching up toward a high decorated gable. Several little screen porches appear upstairs and down.

Norwalk pioneer rancher Darius D. Johnston built the house and lived there with his wife Eudolpha and two daughters Edith and Cora. They raised wine grapes on 120 acres. Darius had helped to organize the Norwalk School District in 1880 and was on its Board until his death in 1917.

Meanwhile, in 1893 Cora married Charles F. Hargitt, whom she met on Catalina Island where he owned a curio store. They came to live in the ranch house also. Their son Charles (known as Chun) inherited the house and lived there his entire life. After having been home to only one family, the Hargitt House was given to the City of Norwalk on Chun's death in 1975.

During Prohibition times, the family began raising citrus, prunes, and avocados. The ranch increased to 167 acres, with tall trees cloaking the house. Today new homes have filled the ranch lands, leaving just the Hargitt House and an even older water tower built in 1878.

You'll use the everyday entrance, through the side porch. The Norwalk Women's Club has refurbished the old house with many items from the Johnston-Hargitt family. The furniture is pleasant and livable, with a rare 150-year old five-legged dining table and ruby glass dishes.

The docents have arranged a "Catalina shelf" in the parlor, to honor the romance of Cora and Charles. There's an abalone shell from 1893 painted with a Catalina restaurant menu, and old postcards of island scenes.

This was a music-loving household, with a 1911 Victor Talking Machine (Victrola) still playing records at the turn of a crank. A stately Guelph organ in the Music Room and a 1931 radio must have been family favorites. Overhead is a combination light fixture, rigged for both electricity and gas lighting.

Upstairs, lace curtains and handmade quilts are tidy luxuries. Downstairs are photos of family members and the former ranch.

Although the house was vacant for about three years after Chun's death, it's back to life now and has a comfortable air. It's not hard to imagine Eudolpha and later her little grandson enjoying Christmas in the lamplight.

How to get there: The Hargitt House is at 12450 Mapledale St. From the 605 Freeway, exit at Rosecrans Ave. and drive east. Turn right on Pioneer Blvd. and left on Mapledale. For open hours, call (562) 929-5702.

Pico Rivera Historical Museum
✧ *Pico Rivera* ✧

HOW DID THE TOWNS of Pico and Rivera get together to become Pico Rivera? Thereby hangs a tale.

First, imagine little settlements sprinkled across the old ranchlands of the San Gabriel Valley. In the Mexican period, this area was part of Rancho Paso de Bartolo (owned by Don Pio Pico) and Rancho Santa Gertrudes (granted to Don Antonio Maria Nieto).

Americans from the East and Midwest first established the village of Gallatin, than Ranchito on lands just west of the San Gabriel River. A store and a post office were enough to make a town in those days, with a blacksmith shop or school following close behind.

Maizeland was the next farming community, named for its high fields of corn. In 1887 Maizeland's Old Barton ranch was subdivided to make the township of Rivera. The town planners vied for the railroad, and soon the Santa Fe routed its eastbound track from Los Angeles through young Rivera. During a "land boom," this was one of more than 100 towns platted in Los Angeles County between 1884 and 1888.

For years, the powerful San Gabriel River roamed at will, zigzagging across its wide floodplain and often cutting new paths. One year a deep channel swept through west of the villages; this is today's Rio Hondo, the deep river, while the main San Gabriel now parallels it on the east. Between the two is Pico Rivera. Miles of irrigation ditches, or "zanjas," once crisscrossed the fields between the two waterways.

Corn and grapes were the first crops in this water-rich area. Rivera was deep in walnuts, which also flourished in neighboring El Monte to the north and Whittier to the east. When that industry declined in the 1920s it was replaced by oranges and avocados.

The community of Pico was following a similar evolution, with church, school and women's club of its own. Pico also had the Los Angeles Eastside Airport, operating from the mid-1920s to the mid-1930s, where young barnstormers practiced such skills as flying upside down and precise mailbag-drops while in flight.

The Whittier branch line of the Pacific Electric Railroad arrived in this area in 1903, with a stop at Rivera. The big red cars continued their runs until 1938.

In the meantime, present day Whittier Boulevard was an informal "line" between Pico to the north and Rivera to the south. Open lands abounded until after World War II. Then change was swift, as orchards gave way to housing tracts. Not until 1958 did Pico and Rivera come together to form one city – Pico Rivera.

This intriguing "family tree of a city" can be traced at the Pico Rivera Historical Museum, now housed in a neat little Santa Fe Depot dating from 1887. Its three rooms are crowded with mementos from this heartland of the valley. Photographs show groves, schools, a landmark drive-in theater for 1200 cars, and the old Stream-land Park, where children rode ponies in 50 shady acres beside the river. Praise to the volunteers who keep such memories alive.

How to get there: The museum is at 9122 E. Washington Blvd. From the 605 Freeway, exit at Washington Blvd. and drive west. Call (562) 949-7100.

Savannah Memorial Park

✧ *Rosemead* ✧

MODERN URBAN CIVILIZATION lies so completely across the Southland that we often do not notice something very old which is right beside us. One example is the Savannah Memorial Park in Rosemead, which has been following its appointed purpose for 150 years.

Geography determined the fate of this small pioneer cemetery. In 1850, a small group of migrants from Kentucky crossed the Cajon Pass and entered the San Gabriel Valley. They settled in an area known as El Monte or "The Monte", a wooded island-like place nearly surrounded by the San Gabriel River. Lush with vines and willows, this watering spot was an important camp for decades of travelers reaching arid Southern California.

Naming the area Lexington, the settlers began a varied agriculture. Theirs was the only non-Spanish white community between Los Angeles and the Mormon settlement of San Bernardino. By 1866 the town had reinstated the name of El Monte and was growing hops, flowers for seeds and English walnuts which eventually covered hundreds of acres.

But the first deaths in the settlement posed a problem. With the concentration of ground water between the Whittier and Montebello hills (the present-day Whittier Narrows) the area was virtually an underground lake. Even a shallow hole immediately filled with water. Some claimed that wooden legs of a table or chair, if poked into the ground, would start to sprout.

Seeking drier ground, the citizens crossed the river and placed their first graves at a point two miles west of El Monte's present Valley Mall. This plot is now called the Savannah Memorial Park. It is still in use and recognized as the first Protestant cemetery in Southern California.

Although operated by the El Monte Cemetery Association, the property has long been associated with early settlers of Rosemead too. In 1867, John Guess of Arkansas began to purchase the 164 acres he would name Savannah Ranch ("savannah" refers to grassland with scattered trees.) In 1872, he donated land for the Savannah School and successfully raised alfalfa, cattle, mules, and horses on his ranch. The surrounding area and town, including the cemetery, took the name of Savannah.

In the 1870s, much of the San Gabriel Valley was a broad pasture, mainly for sheep, with the village of San Gabriel clustered around its mission, and the valley's other main settlement at El Monte. Later Savannah became Rosemead, named for pioneer Leonard J. Rose.

A major wagon trail of those days, an extension of the Santa Fe Trail and route of the Butterfield Stage coaches, came from Los Angeles to El Monte and continued across the Arizona desert. This is present-day Valley Boulevard, now the address of the Savannah Memorial Park.

Today the old cemetery is neat and grassy, lightly shaded by magnolias and deodars. Descendants of John Guess and his eight children still live in Rosemead. The Memorial Park peacefully shelters the pioneers of Savannah and the city it became.

How to get there: From the 605 Freeway, turn west on Ramona Blvd., then angle northwest (right) on Valley Blvd. to 9263 E. Valley Blvd. For background information, call the El Monte Historical Society at (626) 444-3813.

Tongva Outdoor Exhibit
at Heritage Park
✧ *Santa Fe Springs* ✧

HAVE YOU BEEN WANTING to get in touch with the Gabrielino culture, originally called Tongva, which lived so lightly on the land here for centuries? There are two good ways to do this, both at Heritage Park in Santa Fe Springs.

The first way would be to attend one of the weekend Intertribal Gatherings at the park, held at intervals throughout the year. You can call ahead to find out the next dates. There you'll find dancers, basketmakers and storytellers. Shop for arts and crafts, and sample Indian fry bread. The tribes will welcome you.

The second way to experience the Tongva culture is far quieter. In fact, it's so quiet that you can almost hear voices of long ago. This would be to visit the new Native American outdoor exhibit at the park, which is open all year. Dedicated in 1999, this secluded corner seems a peaceful village where

the inhabitants are just out for the day at their tasks. You can imagine they will return.

In the northwest corner of this extensive park is the imaginary village of Chokiish, which might have had 50 homes about 1540. Before the San Gabriel Mission was established, a scattering of villages hugged the streams of the old Southland. Near a river connecting Puvungna (now Long Beach) with Asuksangna (now Azusa) was this spot you've reached. All is quiet there.

Curved "sitting walls" are set into a terraced slope, facing a huge domed house of willow and reeds. The Spanish described these dwellings as being shaped like half an orange. You can step in and rest a moment on woven reed matting. Sunlight flickers into the large space.

Outside a stream rushes down to form a pool, edged with delicious-smelling native sage. Santa Fe Springs had hot springs too, which were social centers for the Tongva people. Nearby a granary holds acorns and at times a bark canoe rests beside the stream.

The exhibit was designed with the help of Tongva descendents. Shells found there during site preparation indicated early settlement and ties with the shore-dwelling peoples. Historic markers remind us that, in 1771, the first San Gabriel Mission was built near here on the San Gabriel River. Soon flooded out there, it was rebuilt in its present spot in 1775.

Whichever way you choose, the crowded powwow or the quiet saunter, don't fail to visit this newest offering at Heritage Park. Then you can pursue your knowledge further in books, or make an annual return for the spirited tribal gatherings.

How to get there: From the 210 Freeway, drive south on the 605 Freeway, then east on Telegraph Road, right on Heritage Park Drive and left on Mora Drive to 12100 Mora Drive. Call (562) 946-6476.

Bosque del Rio Hondo Park

◇ *South El Monte* ◇

THE BOSQUE DEL RIO AREA, along the Rio Hondo River in South El Monte, is rich in human history and also in river history. It's situated within the large Whittier Narrows Recreation Area.

This is a tale of two rivers, actually two strands of the once temperamental San Gabriel River. Life giving and unpredictable for centuries, it has shifted its course many times.

Today the two rivers, running roughly parallel for a while, are called the San Gabriel River and, west of it, the Rio Hondo. Flowing south from the San Gabriel Mountains, the two must pass through a gap several miles wide between the Montebello Hills and the Puente Hills on their way to the sea. This gap is the Whittier Narrows.

Earthquakes and floods used to cause countless migrations of the streams. In flood years, the San Gabriel would leap its banks and wash over adjacent land. Then its old river-bed would fill with silt and willow thickets, and the flow would cut a new channel. Early

settlers in the area saw their fields either flooded or stranded by the fickle waters.

A violent earthquake in 1857 opened the channel now east of Whittier Narrows (the present San Gabriel River). Early in the 20th century, floods formed the Rio Hondo (meaning "deep river") as an overflow channel of the San Gabriel River.

Now the Rio Hondo branches from its mother river just northeast of El Monte, flows through the Narrows, then veers west to join the Los Angeles River, and onward to the sea. Today, these rivers wander no more. They are in captivity and keep to their appointed places.

Human history has crisscrossed this area too. The Tongva people, later called the Gabrielinos, lived along the river for 1,000 years before the California mission settlements were established.

The park trails today are part of the Juan Bautista de Anza National Historic Trail, commemorating the 240 colonists from Sonora, Mexico, led by de Anza, who passed here in 1774 and later reached San Francisco Bay.

In the 1920s and '30s, the natural shores of the Rio Hondo were like a beach, enjoyed by local folks for picnics and swimming. Eventually, urban "progress" crowded and spoiled the willowy riverside haunts.

Fortunately, the Santa Monica Mountains Conservancy, with much community help, has recently reclaimed a good length of the Rio Hondo in the Bosque del Rio park. There are natural stretches of the river, surrounded by trees, thickets, and open scrubland. It's a great spot for bird-watching: some 260 of the 455 bird species recorded in Los Angeles County have been seen here.

The park has a Mission-Revival style entry and picnic tables; then you're off on a web of trails: either the rough paths by the river, or the bikeway more out in the open. With luck, you'll hear the Yellow-breasted Chat somewhere in between, or spot a Western Bluebird before you head back for a picnic brunch.

How to get there: Bosque del Rio is at the intersection of San Gabriel and Rosemead Blvds. From the Pomona (60) Freeway, exit at Rosemead Blvd. and drive south. Call the Mountains Conservancy at (310) 589-3200.

East Whittier Woman's Club

◇ *Whittier* ◇

IT WASN'T A VERY PREPOSSESSING PIECE of real estate: an abandoned brick pumphouse, one room with dirt floors and the tired machinery out back. Also, in 1906 the asking price of $500 wasn't easy to come by.

"We'll take it," said the ladies of the East Whittier Woman's Club. And their civic and sociable activities have carried on to this day.

Whittier began as a settlement of ranchers and farmers in the 1880s, and water was incredibly precious. Without it, the region's citrus-growing would be impossible. The most ingenious minds figured out ways to move this vital resource from place to place. Simon J. Murphy, a businessman from Michigan, was ahead of the rest with his East Whittier Land and Water Co.

From water-bearing land beside the San Gabriel River, Murphy brought water in a redwood flume to a series of pumphouses, including the one on California Avenue and Second Street later bought by the women. When George Chaffey, the engineer who

founded Ontario, improved the system around 1902, the little brick building was abandoned.

The rest of its history belongs to the club, founded in 1901 by 17 progressive women "for sociability and intellectual advancement" in their rural district. For the first five years, they met in members' homes. They gave programs on topics of the day (for example, "Does higher education for women make them better wives and mothers?") and also enjoyed music, friendship, and picnics in the walnut groves.

Then came the clubhouse. The husbands were solidly behind the project and cooked an oyster supper raising $170 to complete the purchase. In 1911 the first electric lights were installed, and in 1912 a player piano arrived. A kitchen and dining room were added in 1923.

A tradition of philanthropy began right away, as the Club contributed mission bells for El Camino Real and, in 1907, helped restore the Pio Pico Mansion in Whittier. Charitable activities were funded by renting the now cozy clubhouse for meetings and weddings. Perhaps the most notable was the wedding of Richard Nixon's parents there in 1908.

What would we have done without the women's clubs in our times of national crisis? East Whittier ladies made bandages and knitted sweaters in World War I and responded to each civic need as the years went by.

Twice they turned over their prized clubhouse to be used as a school. Once was in 1910 when the East Whittier School burned down. Later, after an earthquake had damaged another school, the clubhouse was again used by children for a year. After that episode, the members reported their building was seriously "down at the heels," and they had suffered "their own earthquake" of wear and tear. It seemed almost too much to repair.

But repair they did, with the help of the ever supportive husbands, and today the historic building is going strong as the Club has passed its 100th year.

How to get there: The Clubhouse is at 14148 Second St. (corner of California Ave.) From the 605 Freeway, exit at Whittier Blvd. and drive east; turn left on California to Second. Call (562) 693-5586.

Fred C. Nelles School

◇ Whittier ◇

ALTHOUGH ITS EARLIEST BUILDINGS are now gone, the Fred C. Nelles School in Whittier has logged more than a century of service. As a California Registered Historic Landmark, it has a long and significant past not obvious from its present modern style.

In February 1890, California's Governor R. W. Waterman laid the cornerstone for the Reform School for Juvenile Offenders, soon called the Whittier State School. This was the beginning of a system of reformatories operating today as the California Youth Authority. A crowd of several thousand people gathered to dedicate the four-story brick and stone building (pictured here), as a home for both boys and girls. Before that time, juvenile offenders had gone to prison with adults.

The construction of the original buildings and later the school's payroll brought revenue to Whittier during the economic lows of the 1890s.

In 1916 the girls were transferred to a center in Ventura. And in 1941, the Whittier school was renamed for Fred C. Nelles, its sixth supervisor, who was a native of London, Ontario in Canada. That same year the State Legislature created the California Youth Authority, now a statewide network of schools and conservation camps including Nelles.

In the earliest days, the resident boys were mostly runaways, not criminal offenders but those who had "started down a wrong path." The Sentinel, the school's magazine published by the staff and boys, shows these activities in the 1930s: all the students worked hard at various trades, including the bakery, hospital, laundry, print shop, power house, plumbing shop and many more.

Boys assigned to the school's farm reported collecting 450 to 500 eggs per day from the hens, while the boys disking the citrus orchards brought in 25 to 30 boxes of oranges each week for the students' dining room.

Academic classes were held, and cottages housing about 30 boys each had activities to build citizenship (including a 15-mile hike up to Mt. Wilson). A quarantine for scarlet fever recalls the medical concerns of several generations ago.

Today the Fred C. Nelles School houses about 800 young men ages 13-20 who attend school five days a week all year. Vocational skills are still taught also. Just a few brick structures remain from the 1930s on the 90-acre campus. The old administration building, damaged in the Whittier earthquake of 1987, stood unused and finally was razed, while a new residence wing was added. In 1991 an open house for the public celebrated the 100th anniversary of the school.

Residents of Whittier associate Nelles with another California Historic Landmark: the Paradox Hybrid Walnut Tree. This giant, now spreading nearly 100 feet across, was planted about 1907 on the school grounds by George Weinshank, who worked in the school nursery. In those years, the Whittier State School had leased several acres to the University of California for experiments in walnut culture. Today the tree is a reminder of the farmlands and groves once surrounding the century-old Fred C. Nelles School.

How to get there: For historic information on the school, which is at 11850 E. Whittier Blvd., contact the Whittier Museum at (562) 945-3871.

Leffingwell Ranch Park

✧ *Whittier* ✧

IT'S JUST A SMALL PATCH of green now in Whittier between a shopping center and a school. But look at that name: Leffingwell Ranch Park. What is its story?

This is a story of lemons, and it begins with the visit of Charles W. Leffingwell, a school headmaster from Knoxville, Illinois, to see a Los Angeles friend. In 1888 he bought 500 acres along the La Habra hills, near the village of Whittier. It was the land boom time, and optimism carried the day.

Just then, the ingenious Simon J. Murphy was setting up his East Whittier Land and Water Company. His redwood flumes on trestles brought precious water from the San Gabriel River up to Whittier, its flow seeming to defy gravity. In 1894 the intricate ditches reached the Leffingwell Ranch.

With this water and their own deep wells, the Leffingwells had 100 acres of lemons bearing by the turn of the century. Their ranch, managed by Leffingwell's son Charles, became a model for lemon

production in the La Habra area. It was a self-contained growing-to-shipping operation.

The ranch, bordered with rose hedges, added more lemons and grew many acres of oranges and walnuts too. Though more frost-sensitive than oranges, the lemons were the most successful citrus in that area, for their keeping qualities and long season of bearing.

Leffingwell Ranch developed its own sizable village: cottages for Japanese and American workers, a blacksmith shop, stables, offices, and a large packing house. A long Craftsman-style bunkhouse, shown in photos at the Whittier Historical Museum, was designed by Mary Ranney of the Pasadena firm of Greene and Greene.

Getting the fruit to market was a challenge. Like many landowners and towns in Southern California, they lobbied hard to get the Pacific Electric Railway to extend its line to them. In 1908, the line reached La Habra and had a local stop at Leffingwell's.

More surprises: Standard Oil began drilling wildcat wells on Leffingwell's and other nearby ranches about 1910. These explorations were to change the fortunes of Simon Murphy and his land. (Note that Whittier also has a Murphy Ranch Park now, in a wooded canyon).

In 1923 the Leffingwells set up the Leffingwell Chemical Co. on their land to research and manufacture chemicals and sprays for their orchards. The peak citrus production season for Leffingwell Ranch, a Sunkist affiliate, was 1935-36.

But by the 1950s, the rich green groves were vanishing all along the hills. Soldiers returning after World War II caused a boom in housing subdivisions. In 1953 the Leffingwell Rancho Lemon Association closed when the land was bought for the Whittwood Shopping Center and housing tract. Today only the name is left, no buildings or groves of the old lemon paradise. Leffingwell Creek still borders the remaining patch of green, a pleasant oasis in a busy city.

How to get there: From the San Gabriel River (605) Freeway, exit at Whittier Blvd. And drive east; turn right on Santa Gertrudes Ave. and right on Starbuck Street. The park is tucked behind the public library.

Mendenhall Building, Whittier College
◇ *Whittier* ◇

ANCHORING THE CAMPUS of Whittier College is the handsome Mendenhall Building, now the administrative center. But this two-story Spanish style structure was not always the haunt of presidents and registrars.

The steel-framed, tile-roofed building was finished in 1928 as the Temple of the Whittier Elks Lodge. Just one year later, the Depression forced the Elks to sell the choice triple lot and their elegant lodge.

Nearby was the small but flourishing Whittier College, founded by the Religious Society of Friends (Quakers) in 1887 and chartered by the State of California with an inaugural class of three women and one man.

By 1935 the Elks Lodge belonged to the Bank of America. A local widow, Mrs. O.T. (Lena) Mendenhall, wanted to give the building to the college in memory of her husband. Finally she was able to deed

her La Habra ranches to the bank and the bank deeded the Elks building to the college, costing the Quaker school only about $25,000.

It became the college library and administrative offices. A huge upstairs hall with decorated ceiling was the main reading room (today used by the Education Department), while the ground floor held the Great Hall (now called the Lobby) and offices. A beautiful 20 by 50-foot Oriental carpet was soon added.

The college president at the time was William O. Mendenhall, no relative of the donor. To ease possible confusion, the building was briefly known as Menden Hall, but it soon was permanently named the O.T. Mendenhall Building.

Through the 1930s, the college had no more than 650 students at a time, so the President held Christmas parties for the entire student body in the Great Hall. Now the college enrollment numbers about 1,500.

As you step into Mendenhall Lobby today, you'll find a space of pleasing height, lighted by high arched windows, with a wooden ceiling stenciled in red, green and cream. Short stairways at each end reach Gothic-looking pointed doorways, one leading to an art gallery where students and other artists exhibit their work.

Wrought iron balconies flank the fireplace, and a portrait of the poet John Greenleaf Whittier hangs above. On the mantel below are his lines: "Early hath life's mighty question / Thrilled within thy heart of youth / With a deep and strong beseeching: / What and Where is Truth?"

Another touch of history is the Lou Henry Hoover Collection of Chinese Ceramics, blue-and-white porcelain of the Ch'ing Dynasty shown at each side of the fireplace. The dragon vases and ginger jars are old Chinese forms, patterned with interesting creatures. Lou Henry, later Mrs. Herbert Hoover, spent her childhood in Whittier and was a trustee of the college for nine years.

It is worth a visit, to step past the feathery palms in the entrance garden, and into the graceful building lost to the Elks but gained by generations of students at Whittier's Quaker college.

How to get there: The Mendenhall Building is at 13406 E. Philadelphia St. From the 605 Freeway, exit on Whittier Blvd. and drive east. Turn left on Philadelphia St. to Painter Ave. College information is available at (562) 907-4277.

Sheriffs Museum
✧ *Whittier* ✧

WHY HAS THAT Sheriff's helicopter touched down next to the two "black and whites," patrol cars of the Sheriff's department? Is some urgent law enforcement action going on?

Not likely, since this is a 1966 Sky Knight helicopter , flown over 1,350,000 miles and now resting in peace at the Sheriffs Museum in Whittier. The monumental looking car is a 1938 Studebaker patrol car, its high hood looming like the prow of a ship. Just beyond these two is a modern patrol car, parked vigilantly at the door of the museum.

You can take a close look at each of these intriguing vehicles, and another one: a 1960 Sikorsky helicopter shown plucking up some rash or unlucky hiker in a mountain rescue.

The museum's exhibits cover the Los Angeles County Sheriff's Department from 1850 to the present, 150 years of problems and solutions for the public safety. In that time, there have been 30 sheriffs. As you walk through this history, it won't surprise you that essential equipment for the early sheriffs was a saddle (the horse was not considered equipment). You'll also see a replica of a 19th century office and jail.

You may have a feeling that you are not alone—lifelike mannequins with sheriff's uniforms of many time periods are positioned here and there. They seem to be keeping an eye on things.

Exhibit cases highlight the illegal activities of a century ago and of today. There are some grim realities here, so be forewarned. The Night Stalker, Charles Manson, riots and air crashes that you will remember have all demanded sheriff's action and they are portrayed. Weapons, narcotics, and polygraph machines are all part of a modern deputy's work.

There are photographs of all the sheriffs of this county, with anecdotes about their respective terms. This is like a historical timeline, from a law enforcement viewpoint. Peter Pitchess (sheriff from 1958-82) and Sherman Block (died 1998) are recent sheriffs whose influence has been great. It was Block who dedicated this museum in 1989.

Historic buildings have been associated with the sheriff's work also, and there are photographs of many of them, including the old Hall of Justice in Los Angeles and sheriff's stations old and new, all across the county. A small gift shop offers memorabilia of your visit to this unusual corner of history.

The museum is located on the tree-shaded grounds of the Sheriff's Training Academy, which looks like a campus—and it is: a former high school now adapted for the many branches of sheriff's training. Considering the high-pressure work portrayed in the museum, it's a good thing these men and women have such a tranquil base to organize and learn their skills.

How to get there: The Sheriffs Museum is at 11515 S. Colima Road in Whittier. From the San Gabriel River (605) Freeway, exit at Telegraph Road and drive east. Turn left at Colima Road. For information, call (562) 946-7850.

Trees of Whittier

✧ *Whittier* ✧

WHAT DO YOU KNOW about the Canary Islands? They're a sprinkling of seven islands, volcanic and sunny, just off the coast of Morocco in the Atlantic Ocean. Visited by centuries of voyagers, they also have a beautiful native pine: Pinus canariensis. And this Canary Island pine is now one of the trees of Whittier.

For Whittier, like many Southland cities, has a rich "geography of trees." The earliest were the California natives on the barley ranch of John Thomas, where the Quaker settlement began in the 19th century. Live oaks and sycamores filled nearby canyons, and California pepper trees were planted around the ranch house. Their deep green was striking in the wide open landscape.

Soon agricultural trees were prospering in Whittier. This was one of California's first areas in the citrus industry. Valencias were the oranges that thrived best, and lemons were a juicy success also. Avocados had their day, with the still popular Hass variety originating there.

One giant tree, called the Ganter avocado, produced thousands of fruits in a season and was insured by Lloyds of London. It also provided strong root-stocks for new trees.

Walnuts were important too, as growers tested the most productive varieties. A survivor of that prosperity is Whittier's Paradox Hybrid Walnut Tree, planted about 1907 and now a California Registered Historical Landmark, with its span of more than 100 feet.

Rose Hills Memorial Park in the Whittier hills has fine trees, some dating back to its founding in 1914. And Whittier College (established in 1895) soon developed a handsome complement of trees on its campus.

To learn more about the city's trees, consult a slim volume, "The Trees of Whittier," first published in 1931 by the biology department of Whittier College. A later edition was sponsored by a citizens tree survey committee in 1969. At that time, the authors reported more than 300 tree species in the city.

"There is something about trees that makes people think," said a spokesman for Whittier College in the book. How fitting that colleges should be called "the groves of academe."

Today the city's parks department cares for the trees along the streets, as well as those in the parks. A master plan tells the tree species chosen for each city street. If an individual tree dies, it is replaced with the variety for that street.

"Trees of Whittier" lists the city's tree treasury alphabetically, with street locations for each kind. By consulting the book, you can identify the trees of your neighborhood or look around town for some of the world-citizen trees.

And the Canary Island pines: how did they get to the 11700-12500 blocks of Beverly Blvd. where they form an impressively tall green corridor? Local tradition says that a Mr. and Mrs. Comstock brought the seedlings to Whittier about 1910. They had visited the Canary Islands and admired the lofty pines. Park off the high-speed boulevard, then take a walk under them to enjoy this majestic legacy of Whittier trees.

For information, call the Whittier Public Library at (562) 464-3450 or the city parks department at (562) 945-8200.

Smiley Library, Redlands

Mt. Baldy Visitor Center

✧ Mt. Baldy (Baldy Village) ✧

THE FRONT RANGE of the San Gabriel Mountains is threaded with canyons, and their openings are right next to our cities. The upper reaches hold adventures for hikers, while the canyon mouths are woodsy haunts for picnics or play. Such a spot is Baldy Village, just ten miles from the city of Claremont.

The Mt. Baldy Visitor Center, a ranger station of the U.S. Forest Service, is a good place to begin exploring. This building looks like a little mountain schoolhouse—because it was one. It opened in 1921 with eight students, then an addition was built in 1949. In 1995 the old schoolhouse was dedicated as the visitor center for San Antonio Canyon and the region around Mount San Antonio (Old Baldy).

This massive rounded mountain, white in the winter and whale-gray in the summer, is visible from much of Los Angeles County. Its 10,064-foot elevation makes it the high point of the 50-mile long San Gabriel range. Local Native Americans called it "Joat," meaning snow.

A colorful local history is traced in the Visitor Center displays. Gold seekers tried their luck from 1870 to about 1900, building simple cabins and blasting at the rugged canyon with hydraulic mining. Through the 1920s the Great Hiking Era brought hundreds of hardy walkers into the range, and popular rustic resorts sprang up: Icehouse Canyon Resort, Kelly's Camp, and Camp Baldy.

But the momentous flood of March 1938 wrecked cabins and camps with a 150-foot wide torrent, washing out the canyon-bottom road and ending a chapter of canyon history. Only in 1955 was the present highway completed, with its two tunnels and elevation safely above the stream.

The remains of Camp Baldy have grown into the present Baldy Village, with perhaps 1,000 residents. Some of them commute to jobs in the valley. Their homes are mostly tucked out of sight amidst the pines and cedars.

The Visitor Center holds an "indoor nature trail" to give you an idea of the forests beyond. Other exhibits contain objects and photos from the chapters of canyon history. Outside the entrance is a native plant garden dedicated to Southern California naturalist Elna Bakker (look for her classic nature book, "An Island Called California", for introduction to all you see around you). A well-stocked gift area has books, maps, and lots of activities for children.

Outside, a History Trail is in progress, with some tiny stone buildings, a canvas tent cabin, and a pretty little greenhouse for a watershed restoration program. Also underway is the "Joatngna Project" (using the Tongva word for Mt. Baldy), a sample native village with a willow dome-house, twig granary, and beginnings of other structures. Colorful mountain birds are right at home: the Stellar jay and robin. Picnic tables invite you to linger with the delicious aroma of the cedars.

Before you go, read details of the canyon history in John W. Robinson's wonderful mountain volume "The San Gabriels II."

How to get there: From Foothill Blvd. in Claremont, turn north on Mills Ave., which becomes Mt. Baldy Rd., to Baldy Village. Call (909) 982-2829. Ask about environmental education programs.

Honnold Library
at the Claremont Colleges
✧ *Claremont* ✧

IN A SPACIOUS COMPLEX that has evolved over five decades, the Honnold Library anchors the academic life of the six Claremont Colleges: Pomona, Scripps, Pitzer, Harvy Mudd and Claremont McKenna colleges and the Claremont Graduate University. Honnold is at the geographic heart of the campuses, and its surroundings invite you to take a leisurely walk.

Pomona, the first of the colleges, originally had its Carnegie Library, completed in 1907 and now used for other purposes. But as other colleges joined the cluster modeled on England's Oxford University, a large central library was clearly needed.

William Honnold, a Pomona College trustee and founding board member of the new cluster, pledged $1 million on his 80th birthday in 1946 to launch the project.

Honnold was a native of Illinois, educated in mining engineering and first employed in remote Minnesota iron mines on Lake Superior.

He spent 13 years in South Africa developing interests in gold, copper and diamonds. There he met members of the Mudd family, who would also be prominent in the story of the Claremont Colleges. Another close friend was Herbert Hoover, who later sent Honnold to London and Belgium for relief work in war-torn Europe.

In 1922, Honnold and his wife Caroline settled in Los Angeles because its climate reminded them of South Africa. Honnold became a trustee of Caltech, while his wife was a trustee of Scripps College. When the city of Claremont gave permission to close Eighth and Ninth Streets and to remove an orange grove, the library project was underway.

Noted architect Gordon Kaufmann designed the original building late in his life. His prior work included the Scripps College campus, parts of Caltech in Pasadena, and even the Hoover Dam. During construction, faculties and trustees of each college formed committees to discuss paint colors. Unfortunately, neither Kaufmann nor Honnold lived to see the building's completion in 1952.

At the dedication, Louis B. Wright, director of the Folger Shakespeare Library in Washington, made an address, and the venerable Bodleian Library of Oxford, England, sent a telegram of congratulations.

Additions in the following years have included the Seeley W. Mudd Library, attached to Honnold on the east in 1970, and a multi-tiered stack—known as the Grand Bookcase—which added seven levels of shelving within the three floors of the Mudd Library (the stack is adroitly set within a former courtyard). Honnold/Mudd has also been a pioneer in library automation, beginning computer cataloging in 1960 and bringing the entire library system on-line in 1979.

Claremont is famous for its trees, and you'll see many on a walk around the building. Italian stone pines and oleanders surround the quadrangle to the north. A vista stretches past a memorial rose garden to the south, where a double row of tulip magnolias and a number of live oaks cast a welcome shade. Note the architectural harmony of Honnold and its additions, as seen from the south.

For further information, contact the Library Administration at (909) 621-8045.

The Pitzer House

✧ *Claremont* ✧

ON THE NORTHERN SLOPE of Claremont, the Pitzer House faces the morning sun and eastern peaks as it has since 1912. This picturesque fieldstone bungalow has been called by architectural historian Robert Winter "the finest stone house in Southern California."

The house is secure in its memories now, but this was not always so. To its north, the widening of Base Line Road nipped into the property, and crews are building the Foothill Freeway just to the south. But today the Pitzer House has a new lease on life.

Its story begins with the arrival of Samuel Pitzer, originally from Iowa, who settled in Pomona in the 1890s. His son Lee joined him in the citrus industry and bought his own 200 acres in northern Claremont for lemon groves.

He later reported that the cost of clearing the stones was greater than the cost of the land itself. No wonder Claremont has such an abundance of stone buildings, stone walls and foundations.

Fruit growers believed Pitzer's sandy and cool land would not yield citrus, but he succeeded and pioneered a new region for lemons. In 1911 he hired the Pomona architect Robert Orr to design a home for his family, and they moved in on a Friday the 13th (it was September 1912). That winter a severe freeze set the lemon trees back drastically.

Lee and Blanche Pitzer were active in Claremont civic life. Lee's brother, Russell, was the founder of Pitzer College, and his nephew Kenneth Pitzer was once president of Stanford University.

After Lee and Blanche moved to a retirement home in 1949, the Peairs family owned the house and preserved it well. This family operated the Claremont Nursery on Foothill Boulevard and tended the lemon groves until the late 1970s. A later owner used the house for Claremont Psychological Services. Then it stood in danger, caught between two proposed highways.

But the old property has a new life now, containing the Sunrise Assisted Living residence which opened in 2000. A surprising but harmonious new building, shingle-clad, rises just behind the house and holds the living suites. The old stone garage is now a roofless garden house with overhead trellis, under a huge oak. Landscaping continues with aromatic plants and citrus trees, although the Pitzer groves are long gone.

Preservationists agree that the rare old house looks better than it has in years. Its bedrooms are now offices of Sunrise, a nationwide provider of senior care. The living room, the boulder fireplace and woodwork of oak and walnut all have a Craftsman spirit. Most unusual is the central courtyard, originally open to the sky and to the west until a rattlesnake moseyed in one day. Thereafter the space was glassed in, forming a sunny heart to the house.

Outside the beautifully fitted stones flare outward at the base of the walls. A tile roof and Mission Revival arches complete this one-of-a-kind boulder bungalow.

How to get there: To reach 2053 N. Towne Ave., exit from the 10 Freeway at Towne Ave. and drive north. Contact Sunrise at (909) 398-4688.

Raymond M. Alf Museum of Paleontology

✧ *Claremont* ✧

HAVE YOU EVER been spooked by a set of mysterious footprints? What if they turn out to be 250 million years old? These and many other relics of the long ago past can be seen at the Raymond M. Alf Museum of Paleontology in Claremont, truly a rare spot.

Located at the Webb Schools, this is the only nationally accredited museum on a high school campus. The museum director calls this "a library of fossils," with just about one percent of the collections on display. The fossils have been found and prepared mainly by the students.

These quests began more than 60 years ago, when Dr. Raymond Alf came to the Webb School (then just for boys) to teach math. Searching near Barstow, he and a student found the skull of a new species of fossil pig, or peccary. Hence was born the school's Peccary Society, which has taken generations of students to search for the ancient past. "Speak to the Earth!" said Alf, as students carefully dug and explored. Alf died in 1999, but the annual field trips continue, mainly to Montana, Utah, and the California deserts.

The growing collections needed a home and in 1968 the round two-story museum, designed by Millard Sheets, was opened. The upper level holds the Hall of Life, which traces living things from the first cells to human beings. At the entrance is one of Alf's favorite teaching devices: a tall spiral showing the ages of paleontology with the era of humans just a tiny piece at the top.

The circular Hall of Life holds invertebrates, dinosaurs, mammals, fossil tortoises, and dinosaur eggs. The original peccary skull which started all this hunting is there, as is a skull from the 20-foot tall carnivore Tyrannosaurus rex, and much more.

Below is the Hall of Footprints, the largest such display in the United States. "Who goes there?" the students must have asked. The answer has been reptiles, birds, dinosaurs, camels, elephants, even insects—their prints all captured in the ancient slabs. Much of it is Coconino Sandstone from Arizona. The giant elephant prints came from the Barstow area. The bear-dog tracks, found by Alf and his students in 1964, are the only ones known.

All these creatures walking around millions of years ago and leaving their prints as plain as day: it's enough to give you the shivers. The ancient camel and horse tracks are the most common ones in the Southern California deserts.

Accreditation for this museum was achieved by 10 years of planning and improvements, much of it done by students. (Only about 750 of the nation's 8,000 museums are accredited.) In 1997 the students' discovery of a rare duck-billed dinosaur in Montana, the hydrosaur, drew nationwide media attention.

These young people are still speaking to the Earth, and you can too. Ask about educational programs for all ages at the Alf Museum.

How to get there: The Webb campus is at 1175 West Baseline Rd. Take the 210 Freeway to its end, continue on Foothill Blvd., turn left on Wheeler Ave. and right on Baseline. Call the museum at (909) 624-2798.

Scripps College
◇ *Claremont* ◇

IN 1926, a curious sign appeared by a scrubby field in Claremont, not far from the well-established Pomona College. It read: "Scripps College" and just below "For Women Under Construction."

So began one of the joys of architecture and intellectual life at the Claremont Colleges, a cluster modeled on England's Oxford Colleges. President James Blaisdell of Pomona College (founded in 1888) developed the plan, hoping for the benefits of small colleges grouped like a university around a central library.

In 1924, he coaxed Ellen Browning Scripps, a partner in the Scripps newspaper chain, to be a patron. Nearing age 90, she contributed funds to purchase 250 acres, which now contain the Botanical Gardens, Scripps, Harvey Mudd, Pitzer, and Claremont McKenna Colleges.

After more discussions, she gave $500,000 in stock of the Evening News Association of Detroit, to found "the proposed Scripps College for Women." Blaisdell's "fraternity of scholarship" was launched by adding a women's college.

A graduate of the first Scripps class remembers it like this: 50 freshman students (from around the country) and five faculty members arrived at the campus, which was one vast unplowed field. Toll Hall, a dormitory, was the sole college building in the September sunshine. Two small California bungalows were over yonder. One held the lecture room and the president's office. The faculty conferred in the laundry porch.

The other bungalow was the library, with French class held in the attic. A green shed farther off was dubbed the Science Cottage, where biology experiments were soon underway.

There were no alumnae, so the trustees appointed 50 public-spirited women of Southern California to serve as Honorary Alumnae until the little college could produce some of its own. That first year, all 50 students took a chartered bus to La Jolla to visit small, white-haired Ellen Browning Scripps, who never saw her college but was so interested in all its details.

By its third year, the college had Balch Hall, pictured here, a classroom and administration building designed by Sumner Hunt and Silas Burns. Its Spanish Colonial Revival style was lively and fresh, with pleasant courtyards.

The overall plan for the campus was designed by Gordon Kaufmann in the later 1920s, using a picturesque Mediterranean style. Gardens and lawns link the buildings in harmony. There are large open spaces, suitable for outdoor convocations, and small nooks, shaded by olive trees. The 30-acre campus holds about 75 tree species, a sampling of them described in a Tree Tour leaflet with a campus map. This is one of the loveliest college walks you can take anywhere.

How to get there: From the 10 Freeway, exit at Indian Hill Blvd. and drive north; turn right on 10th St. which ends at Balch Hall and an entrance to the campus. Call the Claremont Colleges at (909) 621-8000. Claremont Heritage conducts occasional walking tours of the campuses including Scripps. Contact them at (909) 621-0848.

Claremont Urban Forest

✧ *Claremont* ✧

THEY'RE A BIT like a group of travelers who have come here from many places and are doing very well, thank you, in their adopted homeland. The street trees of Claremont make an urban forest as varied and beautiful as any in Southern California.

About 23,000 street and park trees appear now on a city database called Treekeeper. These records show the history, health and care of each tree.

This concern is based on a more than 100-year tradition. Six days after Claremont's first town meeting in 1889, a committee asked the citizens what trees they would like planted on each street. Residents wanted a shady Eastern or Midwestern feel to their town. They planted American elms from the East and later trees from around the world. Every region of Asia, Africa, Europe, and Australia is represented, plus the Americas and our California natives.

Today the elms flourish along Indian Hill Boulevard at Memorial Park, making a leafy canopy high above. They form one of two designated historic groves in Claremont.

These trees are rare as well as graceful, since many American elms nationwide have been lost to Dutch Elm Disease. Claremont was the first city in Southern California to plant some disease-resistant hybrid elms.

The city's second historic grove is the eucalyptus stand on College Avenue, east of Indian Hill Boulevard. In 1890, Frank Brackett, chairman of the Street Tree Committee, chose saplings that were at least the thickness of one's thumb. He and Henry Palmer, President of the Trustees of Pomona College, drove an old white horse many times up the avenue, carrying water to the young trees. These were spaced wide apart so people could someday see views of the mountains under their branches.

Years later, Brackett said: "the same pioneers who set out those trees were also planting a college, and both trees and college were to grow to proportions far beyond the dreams of those who planted them."

During the land boom of the 1880s in Southern California, developers planted hundreds of trees, and they often chose the fast-growing eucalyptus, sometimes clustering them in groves to suggest a water source.

In 1944 a Postwar Planning Committee was established to develop city projects for the public good. They created a uniform tree plan for each street, putting in such stalwarts as crepe myrtles and purple plums. A local orange grower watered the trees from his tank truck.

Today one of the oldest of Brackett's eucalyptus trees is almost 50 inches in diameter and one measures 130 feet tall. Along with the historic groves, the city has named nine individual trees as heritage trees, noted for their size, age or historical significance. The town's preservation group, Claremont Heritage, knows the stories behind these and can provide more information about the urban forest. Their office is now in Memorial Park, an ideal place to start your walk and to picnic afterwards in the lacy shade of the elms.

How to get there: From the 10 Freeway, exit at Indian Hill Blvd. and drive north to 8th St. This is Memorial Park. Call Claremont Heritage at (909) 621-0848.

Covina Park

✧ *Covina* ✧

IT WAS TREES, on a March day in 1927, that brought together the citizens of Covina. The project was beautification of the City Park, 10 acres bought by the city in 1921 from the Adams ranch. For some years, the park was dusty and rough, just remains of the old orange groves that had once flourished there.

The Covina Lions Club was a major force in the park's history. They started a Fourth of July picnic tradition there in 1923, with a horse race down unpaved Badillo Street. Later, the Lions built a concrete bandstand for concerts.

In 1927, according to the local newspaper, the Argus, "half a hundred men and women, representing the civic clubs of the city, put over in a big way the planting of trees and shrubs" in the city park. Each group planted two or three trees. The men donned overalls and the ladies their aprons. The shifts of workers changed

during the day, as citizens could spare an hour or two from their usual tasks.

Charles G. Adams, a Los Angeles landscape architect, gave his services to help choose the 383 trees and shrubs. He had also supervised the grounds of the Kellogg ranch in nearby Pomona, now part of Cal Poly Pomona.

The groups planting that day were the Woman's Club, the Business and Professional Women, the Rotary, Lions, American Legion and Men's Clubs, and the Chamber of Commerce. All returned the next day to complete the project.

A photographer caught the sense of fun in the hard-working crew. And who was more proud than the fellow whose planting hole swallowed him as far as his vest pockets? In the background of the picture appears the popular bandstand.

Over the years the park has been a summer haven. The seasonal opening of the plunge was celebrated each year in May with music and picnics. The Municipal Band was first launched in the 1880s, then reborn in 1956 as the present Covina Concert Band. Its musicians play free summer concerts in the park (call to learn the schedule).

Summers at Covina Park also include an evening film festival, family fun nights, and various musical groups. The Lions Club is still active there, and where orange groves once stood, children can play on a historic fire engine or a Cinderella pumpkin coach at the playground.

The park holds many memories, some of them told by local historian Pauline Ott, who remembers as one of the loveliest days of her life stepping off the Santa Fe train from Tennessee in 1919 at age 10. Seeing the San Gabriel valley for the first time, she thought it "a fairyland." She was there for that Fourth of July horse race and she has enjoyed Covina Park ever since.

How to get there: Covina Park is at Fourth St. and Badillo St. From the 210 Freeway, exit at Citrus Ave. and drive south. Turn right on Badillo. Call the Covina Park and Recreation Department at (626) 858-7271, for information on activities at the park.

Historic Smudge Pots
✧ *Covina* ✧

SIGNS OF THE CITRUS INDUSTRY can be found all around us in Southern California, once we start to look for them. You'll find packing houses now put to other uses, and old orange trees still growing in rows between our buildings. And like pieces of "found art," there are the smudge pots.

Properly called orchard heaters, these oil-burning pots were life itself when cold threatened the citrus groves. Spaced along the rows of trees, the pots put out sooty swirls of heat. The perils of the frosts are traced in "Heritage of Gold," the 100-year history of Sunkist Growers (1893-1993).

Orange growers in the Southland formed the Southern California Fruit Exchange, later renamed the California Fruit Growers Exchange. In 1907 their advertising folks suggested the trademark "Sunkissed," later adopted as "Sunkist."

The name was stamped on the paper wrapper of each piece of fruit, and for every 12 wrappers and 12 cents sent in, customers would receive a sharp-pointed spoon for eating oranges out of their skins. Soon, up to 3,000 spoons were ordered each day.

In 1912, the population of Los Angeles was about 320,000 people, the Sunkist exchange shipped over 9 million boxes of fruit (exporting through a sales office in London), and the orange seemed the brightest star in the sky.

Then came the famous freeze of January 1913, remembered for years. Temperatures down to 20 degrees Fahrenheit for several nights damaged about 40 percent of the crop. The production goal of 10 million boxes was reduced to 4 million boxes.

Only the smudge pots could relieve the disaster. Thousands of pots burned out their oil completely overnight and had to be refilled the next day. Local oil refineries ran overtime, producing fuel for the pots. The grove workers faced exhaustion but kept on day and night.

There were serious losses and layoffs that year. But the industry came back with another advertising campaign: "Drink an Orange." Although orange juice was almost unknown in 1916, Sunkist ordered a million glass hand-juicers and offered them for 10 cents as a promotion. They were gone in a year, and soon all America was squeezing. These glass reamers are still-useful relics of our citrus past.

The smudge pots were vital again in the major freezes of 1937 and 1949. Belching their grimy but life-giving smoke, the pots saved much of the crop. Long-time residents of Covina and Glendora remember how their parents stuffed the edges of windows to keep the soot out of their houses.

Almost all the citrus groves are gone now from the San Gabriel Valley. And the pots are not allowed to burn oil in our smog-conscious urban setting. But if you have a rustic yard and an orange or lemon tree, you might acquire a pot—just as a piece of historic backyard art.

Where to find them: Antique stores sometimes have smudge pots. Also consult the Covina Historical Museum (626) 966-3976 or the Glendora Preservation Foundation (626) 335-2078, which once sold the pots to support their projects of saving historic buildings.

Chaffey-Garcia House

✧ *Etiwanda* ✧

OH, THE PEOPLE YOU'LL MEET, when you go visiting historic houses. At the Chaffey-Garcia House in Etiwanda, it will be the handsome and rather amazing George Chaffey Jr. and his energetic family, who came to California in the 1880s.

A chronology of this gentleman's life, summarized by the Etiwanda Historical Society, credits him with founding 12 towns, two counties, and a college, four water companies and several banks. Born in Ontario, Canada, George Chaffey was originally a shipbuilder.

Traveling west with several of his brothers, he and brother William bought a 500-acre sheep ranch in 1881 from retired sea captain Joseph Garcia (who was from the Azores).

Garcia's simple house at the foot of the San Gabriel Mountains had been built in 1874. George moved his family into the house and named the area Etiwanda, after an Indian friend from his native Canada. Today, Etiwanda is the eastern portion of the city of Rancho Cucamonga.

Having established Etiwanda, George and William laid out the nearby towns of Ontario and Upland, started two water companies

and Ontario's first newspaper called the Ontario Fruitgrower, established the original Chaffey College (the campus is today's Chaffey High School), then by 1886 left for Australia and more pioneering there.

George was back in California in 1898 and soon afterward set up a vast water project for the Imperial Valley.

In 1920 at the age of 72, widowed but undaunted, George bought a Hudson automobile chassis and designed himself an early "RV" which he called "Sally Brown," to ramble throughout the West for seven years.

Today the Chaffey-Garcia House is full of family mementos. George had three brothers but only one sister, Emma, and Emma's granddaughter has given the house many intriguing Chaffey items. Well-written labels explain the objects from long ago. Upstairs is an airy "children's room." Behind the house is a reconstructed barn with exhibits and photos.

Preservationists could take note of two good examples set by the Etiwanda Historical Society. They had to rescue the vine-choked Chaffey-Garcia House in 1985 and move it out of harm's way from a proposed housing tract. Negotiations with the developers resulted in "historic mitigation," as the developers donated the house, property for its relocation, and funds to create the barn. Now special events are held in the garden and the barn.

An even more unusual idea is their children's support group, called Emma's Friends. These youngsters have restored the upper room and raised money for its furniture and toys. They must take a delight in Emma Chaffey's doll plates and the vintage gadgets that amused children years ago. Working with their parents on the house and gardens, Emma's Friends will be the next generation to preserve historic places.

When you visit this snug but lively home, look in next door at the little white Etiwanda Congregational Church, built in 1902.

How to get there: The house is at 7150 Etiwanda Ave. From the 10 Freeway, turn north on the 15 Freeway, then exit at Foothill Blvd. and drive east. Turn left on Etiwanda Ave. Call (909) 899-8432.

Lordsburg College Site
✧ *La Verne* ✧

A BOTTLE of Dr. Gunn's Onion Syrup—how's that for a window on the past? This object and more turned up at the Lordsburg College archaeological site at the University of La Verne.

In November of 1995, just north of the university's new library, a bulldozer scooped the earth for a landscape project. But work soon halted, because the bulldozer had turned up the kitchen dump of the old Lordsburg Hotel, built in 1889.

This grand hotel of 130 rooms was the dream of I.W. Lord, who had moved to California from Illinois in 1872. Purchasing 800 acres in the land boom of the 1880s, he planned the town of Lordsburg just west of Pomona. Hoping that the Santa Fe Railroad would make Lordsburg a major stop, some 2,500 people turned out for the land auction.

A fine hotel would be needed, and Lord erected a four-story wonder of English and Swiss styles, with multi-level gables, towers, and verandas on three sides. It was similar to San Diego's Hotel del Coronado. But the boom went bust and the hotel soon had no guests.

Finally a group of German Baptist Brethren, also known as Dunkards, bought the building to create Lordsburg College.

From 1891 to 1919, the structure was both college and residence. The first floor contained chapel, recitation rooms, dining hall, kitchen, and library. Upstairs, one half was occupied by the young men, the other by the young ladies. Professors and their families also lived in the commodious building, a village under one roof. These were the years traced in the dig, which yielded objects from studies and daily life.

For several months, today's students learned rigorous excavation methods as they dug up their own academic past. The teams dug in one meter squares, sifting the earth through fine screens and labeling the location of every find. Part of the site was left untouched for the future. In the labs, students washed, identified and labeled the items.

And what did they find? Bottles and cans, seeds and bones, buttons and a sewing kit, tooth brushes of carved bone, hand-painted china fragments from the hotel, lamps and wicks. Also there were "edufacts" (artifacts of education): chemistry test tubes, pens and nibs, spectacles, art supplies, a pocket watch. A vanished way of life was appearing.

Nearby on campus, the archaeology staff has created a "seeded" or mock site for school children, with artifacts planted for students to uncover. Fifth graders through twelfth graders come to this Youth Archaeology Field School.

In 1927 the old hotel building was finally pulled down. The college was renamed La Verne College, and in 1978, the University of La Verne. Later the university's Wilson Library was built on the hotel site.

The dig into the revealing dump has ended now and the site is filled in with landscaping. Occasionally the finds are exhibited, including the bottle of that once-famous tonic, Dr. Gunn's Onion Syrup.

How to get there: From the 210 Freeway, continue east on Foothill Blvd. Turn right on D St. and right on Third St. to the Library and the campus.

Guasti

✧ *Ontario* ✧

A MEMORY of northern Italy, a village, a company town, glimpses of a once-vast wine region—you should know about Guasti.

This tiny center, begun in 1904, keeps its early nineteenth-century character in dusty quiet, although the San Bernardino Freeway is just to the north and the sleek-looking modern Ontario Airport just to the south. Once this Cucamonga Valley, 45 miles east of Los Angeles, was the largest wine-producing region in California.

But prospects did not look good when Secondo Guasti arrived in 1878 from Italy via Mexico. He worked as a cook in Los Angeles and bought a vineyard in Glendale. But South Cucamonga reminded him of his native Piedmont, a great wine region of northwest Italy. Digging into the semi-desert sands of Cucamonga, he found the underground flows from nearby mountains and believed vines would grow with just this groundwater.

With luck and a prayer, he bought eight square miles of this desert, sold shares of his Italian Vineyard Company (IVC) to his countrymen, built fences to keep out rabbits, and planted nearly a

hundred varieties of grapes. Bringing whole families from Italy, he started his town, Guasti, with its own post office, school, store, clapboard cottages, and a lovely stucco church with curlicue doorway.

Enormous stone winery buildings carried on the work. The colony flourished and soon other wineries clustered nearby. In 1917 Secondo Guasti believed his 4,000 acres formed the largest vineyard in the world. IVC wines were marketed internationally through offices in New York, Chicago and London.

Life in the colony seemed full of zest and fellowship. When you visit, look for the charming memoir "Growing Up in Guasti," by Marcia Stumpf. Among many festivities she reports that, on Columbus Day in 1909, the Guastis gave a barbecue for 1,700 people to raise funds for an English-language night school for Italians in Los Angeles. They chartered a train to bring guests out to the ranch house from Los Angeles and gave gold medals to the best students of English.

In 1924 the Guastis built themselves a 20-room Spanish-style mansion at the village. It had a central courtyard with Italian marble fountain, an aviary, and varied trees around the grounds for shade. Secondo Guasti and his son Secondo II were remembered as paternal but generous to their many workers.

After World War II, grape production in the Cucamonga region steadily declined, from 20,000 acres of vineyards in the 1950s to about 5,000 acres in the 1980s. The Italian Vineyard Company was dissolved in 1946, but the school and church remained active.

Today the J. Filippi Winery holds a shop and tasting room in one of the impressive stone buildings. The rows of worker houses are dormant. But the Guasti Mansion is available to rent for events, truly a special spot. And the dream of Secondo Guasti, which did come true, can still be felt as you explore the peaceful dirt lanes of his colony.

How to get there: From the 10 Freeway, exit at Archibald Ave. and drive south; turn left on Guasti Rd. Call for Guasti Mansion reservations at (909) 605-7677.

Cal Poly Pomona
❖ *Pomona* ❖

THE STORY of Cal Poly Pomona and its 1,400-acre campus is the story of two interesting families who converged in Southern California. For a short time, their names joined in the name of the school: California State Polytechnic College, Kellogg-Voorhis (1966-1972).

Charles B. Voorhis, a native of Kansas, came to Southern California in 1925. He was by then 55 and retired from a successful career first with a plow company, then as sales manager for the Nash Motor Co.

But Voorhis had the welfare of boys on his mind and he had the financial means to help. In 1927 he bought 150 oak-shaded acres in the San Dimas hills, to found a school for homeless boys.

The idyllic campus was a community to which the graduates could always return. Voorhis covered most of the operating costs himself and appointed his son, Horace Jeremiah Voorhis (known as Jerry), to be the headmaster.

Jerry Voorhis was born in Kansas and graduated from Yale. Although he came from an affluent family, he worked for a time in

factories and freight yards. He and his wife had started a boys' orphanage in Wyoming when his father called him west to head the Voorhis School for Boys, which he did for 10 years.

He was elected to the U.S. Congress in 1936 and served until defeated by Richard Nixon in 1946. He continued an active life with educational causes. His son Jerry Livingston Voorhis taught history at Cal Poly for a time.

W.K. Kellogg, the cereal magnate from Michigan, also came to Southern California in 1925 and bought 377 acres for an Arabian horse ranch in the Pomona hills. The likes of Rudolph Valentino and Will Rogers came to ride these gorgeous horses, and the spread grew to 850 acres. The noted architect Myron Hunt designed him a spacious house in the Spanish style.

Meanwhile, Charles Voorhis donated his school to the state in 1938 to become the Southern branch of California Polytechnic College, San Luis Obispo. In 1949, Kellogg deeded most of his ranch to the state for another expansion of Cal Poly, called "the Kellogg unit." The two properties were just a few miles apart.

The final convergence occurred in 1956, when the student body of 550 outgrew the Voorhis site and moved to the larger Kellogg site, creating today's Cal Poly Pomona campus, now with some 17,000 students. The university first admitted women students in 1961.

As a condition of the donation, Kellogg required Cal Poly to continue raising and showing Arabian horses. Kellogg's large ranch home is now a center for scholars and special events.

At the recent dedication of the new Voorhis Park beside the administration building, graduates of the original boys school brought spades of soil from their long-ago campus. And below Kellogg's recently restored mansion is the Voorhis Ecological Reserve, a woodsy hillside threaded with paths through native plants.

How to get there: From the 10 Freeway, exit at Kellogg Dr. and follow it to the campus. To check for plant and produce sales, horse shows, and visits with the animals, call Visitor Information at (909) 869-7659.

Palomares Adobe

✧ *Pomona* ✧

THEY WERE YOUNG, the two petitioners seeking a grant of the former San Gabriel Mission lands in 1837. Ricardo Vejar was 35, his ranching partner, Ignacio Palomares, just 26. Today, you can visit the adobe home built by Palomares for his family and see what the two made of their spacious Rancho San Jose.

Yes, California's Mexican governor Juan Bautista Alvarado did grant them about 15,000 acres (two leagues) embraced by hills and covering the western portion of the Pomona Valley—the cities of San Dimas, La Verne, Pomona and Claremont today.

The northern half of this spread, worked by Palomares, was called San Jose de Arriba (upper). Vejar's southern share was called San Jose de Abajo (lower). The two friends raised Mexican cattle for their hides, tallow, horns and meat. Each had a home which offered the noted hospitality of pastoral California.

The Palomares Adobe was finished in 1854, with 13 rooms in an unusual T-shaped plan. In the short stem of the T was a "sala" or

reception hall, and two bedrooms. In the long north-south wings were the kitchen, dining room and storerooms, three more bedrooms, and a "tienda" or store where Palomares sold ranch supplies. At about 3,500 square feet, the adobe was the largest home in the region and a festive social center.

The house had cloth ceilings, wood floors in the main rooms, and a shake roof. Hence it was called "Casa de Madera" or the House of Wood.

But the 1860s brought dreadful hardships. Floods were followed by two years of drought. Grasshoppers swept through, and then smallpox took a wide toll. Vejar's land was mortgaged, then lost in foreclosure. The property of Ignacio Palomares, who died in 1864, was divided as Americans came to settle the towns of Pomona, San Dimas, and Lordsburg (now La Verne). Fruit orchards filled the former cattle lands.

The Alvin R. Meserve family bought the Palomares Adobe and lived there for 10 years. But eventually the old house was empty. Its bricks slowly crumbled under rains, and one wing was crushed by an overpowering wisteria vine.

The marvel was that in 1939, with the property owned by the City of Pomona, restoration began under the Works Projects Administration (WPA), the Depression-era Federal program that built so many new public buildings. It was rare for them to work on old structures.

Workers molded 25,000 new adobe bricks on the site, largely from the broken old ones, and they re-created Don Ignacio's home in its original shape. Many of his descendants gathered to rededicate it in 1940. The Historical Society of the Pomona Valley cares for it today.

Step in, from the herb garden and the earthen patio. You'll find an intriguing mix of 19th century furniture, two square pianos, camphor-wood chests for storing clothes, imported china and fans, a huge tallow pot and tiny doll dresses: here is the life of a busy early California household.

How to get there: The Adobe is at 491 E. Arrow Highway. From the 10 Freeway, exit at Towne Ave. and drive north; turn left on Arrow. Call (909) 620-0264.

Phillips Mansion
✧ *Pomona* ✧

ONE OF THE FIRST emigrant trails to California came over the
Cajon Pass, through San Bernardino, along a beautiful valley
between the San Jose Hills and Puente Hills, and into the Los
Angeles basin. In that valley Louis Phillips, first resident of the
area after the original Mexican grantees, built in 1875 a brick
mansion which still stands.

Don Ricardo Vejar owned the southern portion of the vast San
Jose Rancho (now the Pomona area) from 1837. But he lost his land
to creditors during the droughts of the 1860s. The new owners hired
Phillips as overseer and in 1868 he bought 10,000 acres of the
property.

Born in Prussia in 1829, Phillips had come to America at age 13
and eventually headed West to work for relatives. Thrifty and honest,
he won the respect and friendship of the Mexican Californians. He
rode over his property (half hills and half lowlands) with a notebook,
observing needs. Once he drove a band of horses as far as Salt Lake
City and sold them for enough to clear his title to the ranch.

He married the vivacious Esther Blake of El Monte, and their family of four children outgrew the small Vejar adobe they occupied (now gone). The three-story mansion completed in 1875 was built of bricks made on the spot, and had gas lighting and a mansard roof. The house was strangely urbane in the California grasslands, being of Second Empire design (named for Napoleon III whose building campaign had once transformed Paris).

Around his home, Phillips oversaw 6,000 sheep, 300 head of cattle and 1,800 acres in barley, wheat and rye. He gradually sold nearby lots to create the village of Spadra, an important transfer depot for coaches, 20-mule freighters, and later the Southern Pacific Railroad heading east. The narrow Spadra Valley (named for Spadra Bluffs, Arkansas) hummed as the midpoint between Los Angeles and San Bernardino.

Later Phillips sold land for the original township of Pomona, incorporated in 1888. As activity shifted to that growing center, Spadra dwindled. Its remains were finally annexed to Pomona in the 1960s.

Louis Phillips died in 1900 at age 70 and Esther stayed on in the French mansion until 1918. The house was in the family until 1931, became an apartment house in World War II, then stood vacant and vandalized. The stagecoach route through the slender valley had become Pomona Boulevard, crisscrossed by the Corona Expressway and the Orange Freeway.

Today the Phillips home is completely surrounded by industrial complexes and was two days away from demolition when the Historical Society of Pomona Valley intervened. Now owned by the city of Pomona, the mansion will be open to visitors when earthquake repairs are complete. Its dignity intact, it awaits supporters who value its long history. In the meantime, college students maintain its grounds and the Historical Society hosts events there.

How to get there: The mansion is at 2640 Pomona Blvd. From the 210 Freeway, drive south on the 57 Freeway and exit at Temple Ave. Drive west; then turn right (east) on Pomona Blvd. Call the Historical Society of Pomona Valley at (909) 623-2198.

A. K. Smiley Public Library
✧ *Redlands* ✧

THE A.K. SMILEY PUBLIC LIBRARY in Redlands has passed its hundred-year mark now, and it has never looked better.

The town itself was platted by the Redlands Water Company in 1887, and two years later two brothers arrived from New York who would bring the community national fame. Alfred and Albert (A.K.) Smiley were identical twins.

All their lives they enjoyed dressing alike and confusing people about their identities. The histories of Redlands show photographs of them, alike in frock coats with trim under-the-chin beards.

They bought 200 acres on a ridge southwest of town and created a botanical park surrounding their two homes. Five miles of scenic roadways wound through lush plantings. Little summerhouses with palm roofs were scattered over the grounds. To this Canon Crest Park came such visitors as Andrew Carnegie, William McKinley and Theodore Roosevelt.

The brothers had been born in Maine in 1828 and were Quaker schoolmasters until their 40s. Then they became proprietors of

thriving resort hotels at Lake Mohonk, New York. A winter visit first brought them to Redlands at age 61. The dry ridge, soon to be known as Smiley Heights, intrigued them right away. "No water? What of it! We will get some." And they did.

The brothers were caring philanthropists: Albert as trustee of the Carnegie Peace Fund and on the National Board of Indian Commissioners—and Alfred as founder of Associated Charities of Redlands. In 1898 Albert gave to Redlands a fine public library set in a park, borrowing much of the $60,000 cost. The architect was T.R. Griffith.

Andrew Carnegie, who gave his own funds for many libraries throughout the U.S., praised Smiley for incurring the debt: "in his love for the cause. . . he has gone further than I have."

The two brothers, who could be told apart by their gold watch fobs, became beloved figures in Redlands. In later years, their civic interests were carried on by their younger half-brother Daniel. Canon Crest Park, much visited by tourists, remained intact until 1962 and then was subdivided.

A.K. Smiley's library is a Moorish/Mission style building, which has been expanded five times since 1898. The additions in 1926 and 1930 were designed by Myron Hunt, the architect of Pasadena's central public library. The newest addition, by Cathleen Malmstrom of San Francisco, was completed in 1990.

Today this is one of the most beguiling of public libraries. A carved stone entrance leads to the large main hall with polished oak floors. A coved ceiling and oak beams shelter the main reading room.

Light seems to flow everywhere, from a stained glass round window, arched windows, and leaded diamond panes. Even the newest rooms carry out the 19th century style. The central square tower was removed in 1936 as an earthquake hazard, but has now been rebuilt in honor of the library's 100th birthday. The original furniture, recently restored, is still in place.

To all who love libraries, this one is truly a gift from A.K. Smiley.

How to get there: The Library is at 125 West Vine St. For information and directions, call (909) 798-7565.

San Dimas Canyon Nature Center

✧ *San Dimas* ✧

THERE IS A STILLNESS in nature around the Winter Solstice. As this celestial turning point approaches (December 21), the sun swings low in the sky and animal activity seems to pause in the long shadows. You can feel this quietness in a winter visit to the San Dimas Canyon Nature Center.

The Center is in 138-acre San Dimas Canyon County Park, in the San Gabriel Mountain foothills between Glendora and La Verne. The first center originated 50 years ago in a little wooden house, now used for storage, which was then home to a caretaker for the canyon's water pump.

Today the Nature Center has a new museum and education building, opened just last spring. Designed by Altadena architect Adolfo Miralles, with 900 square feet it is as snug and versatile as a one-room cabin. The exterior of wood and native stone fits comfortably into its surroundings.

Inside is one ample all-purpose room, with displays along the walls and open space for classes and projects. Adjacent are small

rooms for office, library and a little gift store. Everything will point your interest to the real "nature center", which is the outdoors.

This site is the only Los Angeles County park with an enclosed wildlife sanctuary, sheltering birds and animals that can no longer live in the wild. They stay in enclosures outside, among the oaks – the owls very still in the daytime, an opossum asleep in a boxy "burrow" with a transparent side, a deer moving slowly across its space. These creatures are here because they were injured, or imprinted (bonded) with humans as pets. One deer was found wandering in traffic and rescued. The birds of prey are treated in a special area not open to visitors.

The Center is busy with programs, including a live animal presentation each Saturday (call to confirm this). Children aged 8 – 12 may join the Junior Rangers and those 13- 17 can become Junior Naturalists, trained to help with presentations and care for the creatures. Nature camps are offered during school breaks and summer. Volunteers also visit hospitals, schools, and fairs to share their knowledge and love of the wild world.

Opposite the new building's front door begins a one-mile loop trail, rising gently from an oak woodland, then along a chaparral-covered slope. Here the little ground birds are active, towhees and juncos. As you climb, there's a fine view of the surrounding hills, a wild topography that spreads out around you. If you have children with you, watch out for the spiny opuntia cactus here and there along the route.

You can end, or start, your visit with a picnic in the large grassy park just south of the Nature Center. Its live oaks, playground, and dozens of tables invite an outdoor lunch.

How to get there: From the 210 Freeway, continue east on the 30 Freeway and exit at San Dimas Ave., drive north, then east on Foothill Blvd. and north on San Dimas Canyon Rd. Angle left on Sycamore Canyon Rd. to reach the Center. Call (909) 599-7512.

San Dimas Mansion

✧ *San Dimas* ✧

SO MUCH DEPENDS on the "Boom of the Eighties," Southern California's surge of activity and optimism in the 1880s. Whole towns started up and railroads crisscrossed the area, with Southern Pacific and Santa Fe in competition for customers. Many towns have some evidence left from those hectic times. A choice example is the San Dimas Mansion.

In 1887, the Santa Fe Railroad was extending its line from San Bernardino to Los Angeles. Moses Wick of Pomona organized the San Jose Land Company to plat a new town on the route, called San Dimas. As land values boomed, this was one of 25 town sites between San Bernardino and Los Angeles, two cities only 36 miles apart.

Like the land development on a huge Monopoly board, hotels sprang up to anchor the new towns. Most of these impressive inns are now only memories. They were meant for the railroad travelers and real estate buyers. But they were also icons of prosperity, built on a grand scale though surrounded by vacant lands.

The San Dimas hostelry was designed by Joseph C. Newsom in the Eastlake style, a variation of Queen Anne architecture. Along the roofline are the seven chimneys of its 14 fireplaces. The highest tower reaches to 65 feet, while the veranda, 100 feet long, faces east to catch the morning sun. The redwood building encompasses 13,200 square feet.

But the land boom was over by 1888. Speculation had collapsed and a drought just made matters worse. The San Dimas town enterprise sold only 12 lots, and the hotel never had a paying guest.

In 1889, J.W. Walker of Covington, Kentucky, bought the building and six generations of his family lived there until 1978. During these years, the mansion was a benevolent centerpiece for the town, used at times for a school house, a club meeting place, a church and a venue for weddings and funerals. It is now listed on the National Register of Historic Places.

This is the last survivor of three hotels built by the San Jose Ranch Company along the Santa Fe line. One was at Lordsburg (now La Verne) and became the early home of La Verne College. The other was also in La Verne but it too has vanished. The San Dimas Hotel had the fortunate fate of becoming a family home, so it lasted into the 20th century.

In 1889, Alonzo Davis, a Los Angeles county supervisor, reported that 60 ghost towns founded after 1887 remained on the assessor's rolls. Alosta, Gladstone, Raymond, Sycamore Grove—all are gone now. But San Dimas held on through the hard times and developed a thriving citrus culture.

Today the sunburst designs on the San Dimas Mansion recall the exuberant land boom. New uses are planned for this fine old survivor, including offices for the San Dimas Historical Society and for the Festival of Western Art.

How to get there: The Mansion is at 121 N. San Dimas Ave. From the 210 Freeway, exit at Arrow Highway and drive east; turn left on Bonita Ave. and left on San Dimas. Call the Historical Society at (909) 305-9466.

Sipple Building

✧ *San Dimas* ✧

IN SAN DIMAS, the year 1904 was going to be a good year for business. The first telephones were installed in town that year. The Citrus Union (the first fruit packing house) and the Lemon Association had a combined membership of 126 growers. There were plenty of customers for a new hardware enterprise.

The Sipple brothers of Azusa built their two-story brick building on a prominent corner of unpaved Bonita Avenue, the main street. The business section was about two blocks long and shaded with trees. A few years later, hitching posts were installed along the side streets.

The Sipple Building sold hardware as well as wagons, carts, harnesses and plows. The second floor was divided into eight apartments as the San Dimas Rooming House.

The little community had first been known as Mud Springs, for its natural water source that had attracted such travelers as the explorer and trapper Jedediah Smith, passing through the valley with

his men in 1826. You'll see the name of Mud Springs on early maps. The Santa Fe Railroad came through in 1887, stirring the land boom that shook up all of Southern California.

Farther back, the area had been a part of the Rancho San Jose, a Mexican land grant given to Ignacio Palomares and Ricardo Vejar in 1837. Vestiges of that sweeping property were operated as the San Jose Ranch Company for many years.

Meanwhile the R.M. Teague Nursery (now gone) just down Bonita Avenue from the Sipple Building, became the town's premier business. The Teagues grew citrus trees, more than 200,000 per year by 1920, and shipped them around Southern California, to other states and even to foreign lands with citrus-friendly climates.

All these operations needed hardware, and the Sipple Building had four shops with various occupants: dry goods, a vegetable and grocery store, a butcher shop, and a soda fountain. In 1919, the San Dimas Press moved in for a time, publishing the town newspaper founded as the Eagle in 1903.

Other occupants in the versatile building over the years were a jewelry store, the Los Angeles County Building Department, and for nearly 20 years a United States Post Office.

Several years ago the well-worn building was completely rebuilt, using the original bricks for its face. Studying an old photograph, you'll see it looks just the same. There are now 12 apartments upstairs for senior citizens. Downstairs, the flooring of the entrance is the original wood.

A short walk along Bonita Avenue today, starting at the Sipple Building, will take you past antique dealers with a country flavor and to the refurbished Martin House, which holds the San Dimas Historical Society, the Chamber of Commerce and the Festival of Western Arts. All of this makes an enjoyable saunter for a sunny day.

How to get there: The Sipple Building, now San Dimas Hardware, is at 201 W. Bonita Ave. From the 210 Freeway, exit at Arrow Highway and drive east; turn left on Bonita. Call the San Dimas Historical Society at (909) 592-1190.

Teague Grove

✧ *San Dimas* ✧

THE TEAGUE GROVE in San Dimas is no bigger than a memento: it's about a dozen fruit trees blooming and fragrant in the spring, planted not far from the City Hall. The grove commemorates a large family and a very large business—one of the largest citrus nurseries in the world, which flourished for years along Bonita Avenue in San Dimas.

It all began with Crawford Pinkney Teague, who came from Iowa to California in 1865 with his four sons and four daughters. After a brief stay near Sacramento, the family settled at Mud Springs (now San Dimas), a watering spot in the sparse landscape of the San Gabriel Valley.

Their early years were a checkerboard of fine and lean, trying acres of grain, with meager water supply or with late spring rain spoiling the wheat and hay. Eventually the area developed reliable irrigation. The time was ripe for the "treasure of green and gold," the citrus industry.

C.P.'s son, Robert, leased land from his father and started about 10,000 young citrus trees in 1889. Local records show

he had nearly 250,000 trees by 1920. Their peak business years were probably 1910-12, with sales up to $100,000 a year. Trees from the R.M. Teague Nursery were shipped across Southern California and to other "green and gold" states—Florida, Texas, Arizona. Teague's trees went also to Italy, Spain, North Africa and South America.

But all was not utopia, not in any form of agriculture. The San Dimas Board of Trade printed 5,000 booklets advertising San Dimas as frostless—then a fateful night came in January 1913. The Teague Nursery trees were covered with ice and were lost by the thousands. Orange production recovered, but the lemon industry suffered a three-year hardship before times were good again.

R.M. Teague was noted for his calm in the face of such disasters. San Dimans remembered him driving about in his Pope-Hartford, one of the few automobiles in town.

The Teague Nursery was a major employer in the area. Early photographs now in the San Dimas Historical Society show trees from the nursery being loaded on Southern Pacific boxcars.

Some Southern Californians remember the tall white stucco façade of the nursery, on Bonita Avenue. Its open gateway led to neat rows of young trees shaded under laths. After the nursery changed hands and eventually closed, the façade remained as a local landmark and was taken down only recently.

Post-World War II development later filled the acres of the nursery. But the enterprises of this pioneer family were immortalized in a local poem: "Here's to the Teagues, who farmed by leagues, all the land now owned between us—And mowed their hay, where the Santa Fe, laid tracks into San Dimas."

How to get there: The Teague Grove is beside the Martin House, 246 Bonita Ave. From the 210 Freeway, exit at Arrow Highway and drive east; turn left on Bonita. For more information, call the San Dimas Historical Society at (909) 592-1190. Their offices are in the Martin House.

Live Oak Park and Southern California Parrots

✧ *Temple City* ✧

YES, THEY ARE PARROTS! Visitors and residents alike may look to the sky in disbelief, as the chunky green birds pass overhead with vigorous squawks. These naturalized citizens of the air are a common morning and evening sight in the San Gabriel Valley.

In 1994, Kimball Garrett, Ornithology Collections Manager of the Los Angeles County Museum of Natural History, began the Parrot Project to study these birds in the Southland's "suburban jungle." He and his teams wanted to know where they came from, how they live, and how many there are. Similar projects are underway on the flocks in Orange County, Bakersfield, Redlands, and Telegraph Hill in San Francisco.

Stories abound about how these exotic birds arrived in our local trees. Some say a pet shop fire freed parrots years ago; others, that they escaped while being smuggled in illegally; others, that they simply migrated here from Central and South America. The researchers believe it may be all of these.

The Amazons are the most common parrots, with big blocky bodies and squared tails. Their wings don't go above the horizontal when they fly. They tend to be named by coloring: Red-crowned, Lilac-crowned, Blue-fronted, etc. Also up there are the parakeets, with slender bodies,

pointed tails, and flappy flight. In smaller numbers are cockatoos, macaws, budgies, and cockatiels, all adapted to the wild. Some field guides now include these naturalized birds (such as the National Geographic Society "Field Guide to the Birds of North America").

The parrots roost in flocks of hundreds, moving as the seasons change. In the spring they break into smaller roosts. They favor broadleaf evergreen trees and eat their fruit. Sweet gum, sycamore, eucalyptus, fig, and cedar all attract them. Curiously, parrots don't nest in our wild land (foothill canyons, for instance), preferring urban groves.

Why have these birds become such successful colonizers here? The San Gabriel Valley is a mecca of street trees and fruit trees for them. Also the many buildings, power lines and poles, radio towers, etc. provide nest sites and roosts.

Researchers attempted a census of the birds in September 1999 and counted 1,150 parrots in the flock around Temple City's Live Oak Park, one of their favorite haunts. About 200 parakeets were there also. More parakeets were at the Huntington Botanical Gardens and the Los Angeles County Arboretum in Arcadia, where they like the Silk Floss trees.

To encounter these birds in full force, serious birders will go to the vicinity of Live Oak Park early, around 6 a.m., as the parrots disperse to forage for the day. The park is also a pleasant spot for family fun, with a recreation center and plenty of lawn to play frisbie or practice cartwheels. All ages will enjoy spotting the feathered friends as they scatter across your neighborhood with their wild cries.

How to get there: Live Oak Park is on Bogue St. just east of Baldwin Ave. From the 210 Freeway, exit at Baldwin and drive south; turn left on Bogue. Read more about the Parrot Project on its website or contact the Pasadena Audubon Society.

Chaffey Communities
Cultural Center
✧ *Upland* ✧

IT WAS A LAND of dreams, where buyers once flocked to buy property and a winter sun gently toasted the new villages. Today this bountiful area just east of the Pomona Valley holds the so-called Chaffey Communities: Ontario, Upland, Montclair, Rancho Cucamonga, Etiwanda, and Alta Loma.

The energetic Chaffey brothers, George and William, established towns and developed irrigation here for several years, then departed in 1886 to develop Mildura, Australia. (Read more about them under the Chaffey-Garcia House.) A group of investors bought their land and formed the Ontario Land and Improvement Company. They created 10-acre parcels, intended to be self-sufficient ranches. Their plan forms the basic grid of streets in today's Ontario and Upland.

But there was no lack of ambitious souls, setting up towns on these fertile lands. Some of their settlements glowed briefly, then went out or melted into stronger towns. Their stories are like a tapestry of hopes.

Consider the towns of Eswena, Marquette, Rochester, and Grapeland, once as well known as Ontario or Cucamonga. The pioneers of Eswena were Dunkards (Church of the Brethren) from Kansas, who settled mainly in Lordsburg (now La Verne). They put out a colony of six families on a nearby tract and named it Eswena, combining the names of three prominent colonists: Eshelman, Wells, and Nair. Despite recruiting trips back to Kansas for more settlers, the village disappeared, blending into Alta Loma and Lordsburg. There the Dunkards founded Lordsburg College, now the University of La Verne.

Like Ontario and other new settlements, Marquette was named for its founder's hometown. In 1887 Edward Fraser of Marquette, Michigan, formed his townsite between Ontario, known as the Model Colony, and Cucamonga, compared to the Garden of Eden for its beauty. Excursion trains brought buyers who picnicked at the land auctions and listened to booster speeches.

Unfortunately the town's vineyards, just starting out, were spoiled by rabbits and drought only two years later, and the citizens of tiny Marquette moved on. Only the pepper trees remain today. The villages of Rochester and Grapeland also disappeared from view, while the luckier towns held on to become today's cities.

Records of all this history, from 1880 to the present, are kept by a thriving organization, the Chaffey Communities Cultural Center. Their museum is in the former Fruit Exchange, now the Cooper Regional History Museum. Meanwhile, their five-acre site in north Upland hosts cultural events, lectures, and concerts. You can rent the site for your own special event.

The centerpiece here is St. Mark's Episcopal Church, designed by Arthur Benton, the architect of Riverside's Mission Inn. Its medieval English look and good acoustics make it a surprising little gem. It was moved to this location in 1966 from downtown Upland. Around it is a two-acre citrus grove. Someday a grove house with outbuildings may join the trees, creating a living history ranch for visitors and recalling those idealistic days when towns were born.

How to get there: The Cultural Center is at 525 W. 18th St. From the 10 Freeway, exit at Euclid and drive north; turn left on 18th St. Call (909) 982-8010.

Cooper Regional History Museum
⬧ *Upland* ⬧

IT'S A NEAT LITTLE ART DECO STRUCTURE, built in 1937, with an intriguing past and a promising future. Its past was citrus and its future, history: for this is now the Cooper Regional History Museum in Upland.

The building was once the Ontario-Cucamonga Fruit Exchange (also called the O.K. Fruit Exchange), which handled fruit for most of the citrus packing houses in western San Bernardino County. This business belonged to the even larger California Fruit Growers Exchange, later known as Sunkist.

By the 1890s, Southern California citrus growers knew they needed to cooperate, to pool resources and control their sales and marketing. The Ontario Fruit Exchange was formed in 1895 and lasted to 1980, riding on that beautiful 20th century dream of "Oranges for Health—California for Wealth" (a slogan of the Southern Pacific Railroad.)

In 1936 the O.K. Fruit Exchange represented more than a dozen packing houses and was selling about 3,000 railroad cars of fruit per

year. It had outgrown its little brick office, and so the architect William W. Ache designed a modern new building. Ache was a specialist in buildings for the citrus industry, including the huge packing houses, a few of which still survive.

He used the popular Art Deco style, inspired by the Paris International Exposition of 1925. This architecture celebrated progress and industry, with clear geometry, stylized ornament and modern materials such as reinforced concrete. Ache created a practical structure holding offices, board room, and storage for many years of records. The community loved it. The Santa Fe Railroad depot was just across the street (and today is a stop on the Metrolink).

After World War II, the citrus industry waned, and the exchanges gradually merged with each other or closed down. The O.K. Fruit Exchange lived its final days near Riverside, and the Art Deco building was used by a Board of Realtors, handling sales of some former citrus lands. Then in 1997, it was named an Upland Historic Landmark and the trim little structure became the Cooper Regional History Museum.

This small but lively center of historical knowledge was named for Ada Ann Cooper, a community leader who left her entire estate to local charities. Her gift of one million dollars turned the exchange into a modern museum, well renovated, with exhibit, library and office space.

The museum is devoted to preserving and interpreting the history and culture of Upland, Ontario, Montclair, Mt. Baldy, and Rancho Cucamonga, from 1880 to the present. Upland, originally called North Ontario, took its name of Upland in 1906. With Ontario, it shares the north-south Euclid Avenue as its beautiful tree-lined main street, laid out by George Chaffey in 1882.

In the museum you'll find historic photos and also the culture of today (recently, an exhibit of original citrus crate labels by school children, with themes of Star Wars and patriotism: the past meets the present!)

How to get there: The museum is at 217 East A St. From the 10 Freeway, exit at Euclid and drive north one mile; turn right on A St. Call (909) 982-8010.

Glendale Train Station

Gordon R. Howard Museum
✧ *Burbank* ✧

To EVERYONE who has thought that Burbank is just the name of an airport, you are in for a surprise. A city that began quietly among orchards, later had a romance with the movies and then with pioneering aircraft. This distinctive story is chronicled very professionally at the Gordon R. Howard Museum, home of the Burbank Historical Society.

The city is named not for the botanist Luther Burbank, but for Dr. David Burbank, a New England dentist who settled in the area. He raised sheep there, and later acquired parts of Rancho San Rafael and Rancho Providencia which form the present city.

In the land boom of the 1880s, he sold his holdings to speculators who laid out a town called Burbank and offered small farms and lots. The city was incorporated in 1911 with a population of 500.

The rich valley land produced grapes, apricots, peaches, melons, walnuts, sweet corn, chickens and turkeys. Then the ranches began to sprout movie studios: Warner Brothers bought huge acreage in

1926, followed by the Columbia Ranch (1934), Walt Disney Studios (1939) and NBC (1951).

In 1928 the brothers Allan and Malcolm Loughead arrived. They had built their first seaplane and flown it off San Francisco Bay in 1912. (This was just nine years after the Wright Brothers' pioneering flight at Kitty Hawk). In Burbank, they re-spelled their name as the more pronounceable Lockheed and continued building their wooden flying machines. Their first all-metal plane was constructed in 1934.

The Lockheed Company gave the museum the display materials for their own history, from the carefree "plane relay races" to the serious gratitude of Sir Winston Churchill in World War II. This is quite an enthralling story, full of the dramas of daring people and how mankind has taken to the air.

The Burbank airport, established in 1930 as United Airport, was the largest one in Southern California for several years. In 1979 (after some other stages of ownership) the cities of Burbank, Glendale and Pasadena purchased it and gave it all their names.

This modern stone museum also has a large section of vintage vehicles. You'll walk around a 1928 Harley-Davidson motorcycle with sidecar, a Moreland Motor Company bus built in Burbank in 1922, and ritzy cars such as the Apperson Jack Rabbit and the Thomas Flyer. A huge array of old business machines and vintage cameras may have your head spinning. It's a bit amazing to find the ones you used to use.

The town is documented with photographs, maps, characters and costumes (one is a wartime wedding dress made from a silk parachute). At the beginning or end of your visit, stop just behind the museum at the Mentzer House, pictured here, which is part of the museum complex. This cozy cottage was one of six built in 1887 by the land development company and has been fixed up with choice items of long ago.

How to get there: the museum is at 1015 W. Olive Ave. in George Izay Park. From the 5 Freeway, exit at Olive and drive south. Call (818) 841-6333.

Stough Canyon Nature Center
✧ *Burbank* ✧

A NEW NATURE CENTER is always cause for celebration. The foothills of our local mountains have a generous handful of them—at Eaton Canyon, Placerita Canyon, and San Dimas to name a few. Among the newest, opened in 2001, is the Stough Canyon Nature Center in Burbank. (Stough rhymes with "brow.")

Each of these nature center buildings has its own way of relating modern architecture to the surrounding wild landscape. The Stough Center, designed by Ron Yeo, sits high in a steep-sided niche of the Verdugo Mountains. Facing south, it welcomes a glow of solar energy.

The 4,000 square foot center is tucked among native oaks and sycamores, their branches artistically visible from inside through tall windows. The building is an octagon with its segmented roof floating at interesting angles. Visitors first cross a wooden bridge over a rocky cleft, then reach a tall bronze sculpture which is a dripping fountain. Its carved surface is covered with creatures

and small children discovering them. Hummingbirds may be hovering near the gentle spray at this delightful work by Andrea Favilli.

The building holds an exhibit hall, centered on a "tree of life" showing local habitats such as chaparral and southern oak woodland. Nearby are a classroom, library, workroom, kitchen and offices. By the entrance is a collection of colorful walking sticks, decorated by the junior docents for hikers to borrow and return.

Outdoors behind the center is a round amphitheatre, then footpaths take off into the canyon. These reach up to connect with other trails in the Verdugos, a 10-mile long range across the eastern San Fernando Valley, stretching from Sunland to Glendale. The little center is a gateway to a natural world.

A full schedule of programs is planned for the different seasons: nature walks, birding, crafts and workshops, full moon hikes and canine hikes. Groups may sign on for nature field trips, and children aged 8 to 14 may become junior docents. Admission to the center is free, although some programs have fees.

This property once belonged to Oliver J. Stough, whose ranch and orchards covered the slopes and lowlands below. He purchased 2,000 acres in 1893 from Dr. David Burbank, the area's original landholder. A little city called Burbank was incorporated in 1911, and four years later Stough gave some of his land for a city foothill park. He also provided funds for extending the Big Red Cars of the Pacific Electric line from Glendale into Burbank.

Today the farmlands of Burbank are gone, but the canyons still hold the gift of the wild. The walls of the Stough Canyon Nature Center carry quotes to ponder, including this one from John Muir: "In every walk with nature, one receives far more than he seeks."

How to get there: From the 5 Freeway, exit at Alameda Ave. and drive north; turn left on Glenoaks Blvd., then right on Walnut Ave. into the hills, all the way to the end. Call (818) 238-5440.

Goode House

✧ Glendale ✧

"IT'S STILL THERE!" Preservation-minded people love to hear these words. Often there have been small miracles if a neat old building has survived. In this case there was much human talent too.

Still with us is the Goode House in Glendale, now surrounded with new life. The house is in Queen Anne/Eastlake style, built about 1894 and purchased in 1904 by Edgar D. Goode. He was an Indiana native who came to California in 1882.

Settling into Glendale, he soon became vital in its civic progress. As a school board member, he organized the Glendale Union High School District. He was a County Road Commissioner, and was one of the first to advocate incorporating Glendale as a city, accomplished in 1906.

In transportation, he worked with Leslie C. Brand and Henry Huntington to bring inter-urban electric rail service to Glendale. A web of streetcar lines linked the town to Eagle Rock, Verdugo Park, Montrose, then to Los Angeles and beyond.

His cottage on Cedar Street was a little Victorian gem, just 36 feet wide and 40 feet long. Its wooden exterior has many shapes: bay win-

dows, square covered porch, tower (a Queen Anne feature), and ornamental trim. The roofline has gables and angles galore, and the pointed tower roof has alternating diamond and fish scale shingles.

But the house became a dilemma in recent years. It was one of the few Queen Anne/Eastlake buildings left in the entire city, yet time and neglect almost swept it away.

Various proposals to move or restore the house fell through, usually for economic reasons. The cottage seemed even more tiny among the tall buildings of modern Glendale.

At last the city purchased the property with its triple-sized lot in 1992. A creative plan for re-use was underway when the Northridge earthquake struck in 1994. The cottage collapsed off its four-foot foundation, looking like a child's toy squashed in careless play. Now what?

The house was to be saved, and that was that. The city's Department of Community Development and Housing pressed on, collaborating with the Crippled Children's Society. Edgar Goode's home was to be restored, then surrounded by a 25-unit apartment building, providing affordable housing for disabled low-income residents.

Today you will see the U-shaped building, known as Ivy Glen Apartments, with three stories at the back and one story at the front. The new wood-framed building harmonizes fine with its 100-year old centerpiece. The curved paths in the landscaping are actually ramps graded for wheelchair access. In 1995, the housing opened.

The Goode family home serves as a community center for the residents. It is "back from the brink," its foundation rebuilt and exterior painted. The interior has original or replicated fireplace, moldings and hardware. A man for progress, Edgar Goode would have loved the determination that saved his house.

How to get there: The property is at 119 N. Cedar St. From the 134 Freeway, exit at Glendale Ave. and drive south. Turn left on Wilson Ave. and right on Cedar.

Grand Central Air Terminal
◇ *Glendale* ◇

PERHAPS IT WAS LESLIE C. BRAND who started it with his April Fools party in 1921. Certainly he made a stir among the early airplane people, fliers and dreamers, with his startling invitation to lunch. More than 100 guests came from the movie world, the military and business, despite this catch: they all had to fly in.

The gathering was held at Brand's private air strip. He was Glendale's major businessman and civic promoter whose beautiful white Moorish home is now the Brand Library. It was just 18 years after the Wright Brothers' pioneering flight at Kitty Hawk, and America was in love with flying.

Soon some venture capitalists bought 175 acres for an airport in a more level part of Glendale. The land is between the Verdugo Hills and Griffith Park, beside the Los Angeles River. In February 1929 the spiffy white-towered Grand Central Air Terminal was dedicated there. For the next 30 years, it would host aviation history.

Imagine the early flying machines at this airport: the crackerbox Airster, built there for Amelia Earhart; the biplanes and mail planes; crafts called the flying bathtub, the folding flivverplane (the pilot could fold or open the wings in five minutes), and the Crosby racer based on the aerodynamics of flying fish.

Yes, these were glory days at the Glendale field. Air rodeos drew crowds as wing-walkers and stunt fliers dared the skies. Celebrities loved this heady stuff—Wallace Beery, Gary Cooper, Jean Harlow and Hoot Gibson had been at the gala opening—and the terminal began a short but glamorous life.

In 1933, the 30th anniversary of the flight at Kitty Hawk, this field welcomed the relatively huge Douglas DC-1, which had retractable landing gear. In 1934, Grand Central became a port of entry with regular plane service from Mexico City. That year, Howard Hughes rented a two-car garage nearby and started the Hughes Aircraft Co.

20th Century-Fox filmed Shirley Temple in a movie called "Bright Eyes" at Grand Central in 1934. The pilot-hero of the movie later dropped Christmas presents into her back yard by parachute for years.

As wartime approached in 1939, the first class of Air Corps cadets trained beside the terminal. In 1942 a squadron of P-38s occupied the field to defend Los Angeles. The fighter planes peeled in for landings, low and fast over nearby homes. The P-38s made up 90 percent of the air traffic at Glendale for most of the war. The field was disguised by painted camouflage to resemble a housing tract, and even the terminal building was weirdly blotched with green.

But after the war, planes outgrew the airport, taxes were rising, and Grand Central closed in 1959. Today the airfield is the Grand Central Business Centre, an area of light industry. The white-towered terminal, still decorated with wings and symbols of flight, now belongs to the Walt Disney Co. and sits dormant, awaiting renovation and some new life.

How to get there: The Terminal is at 1310 Air Way. From the 134 Freeway, exit at San Fernando Rd. and drive north. Turn left on Sonora Ave. and left on Air Way.

Southern Pacific Railroad Depot
✧ *Glendale* ✧

YES, IT'S FINISHED NOW—the restoration of Glendale's 1923 Southern Pacific Railroad Depot. If your travels take you north or south, to Santa Barbara or San Diego, you can depart on Amtrak from this little gem of historic architecture.

Its story begins in 1876, the nation's centennial year, when the Southern Pacific Railway completed its line between San Francisco and Los Angeles. The Glendale depot was placed in nearby Tropico, one of the villages on rich farm land between the Verdugo Hills and the Los Angeles River.

Soon Tropico strawberries were selling as far away as New York and Philadelphia. In the prosperous town, some spoke of annexation to Los Angeles, some to Glendale, and some favored independence.

Tempers sometimes ran high on this subject, and after one vote the local paper ran the headline "Jane Tropico Declines John Glendale's Proposal of Marriage."

But settlements were merging all over Southern California: Alosta disappeared into Glendora, Lamanda Park disappeared into Pasadena, and at last Tropico joined with Glendale in 1918. Soon after, perhaps with a nod to its "tropical bride," Glendale chose the hibiscus for its official flower.

In 1923 a new depot, in Spanish Colonial Revival style and designed by architects MacDonald and Cuchot, was built on the site of the old one. For a while, eight passenger trains stopped at the depot daily, and it was the setting for Hollywood films. In its heyday it illustrated the romance of travel, the lure of California.

But eventually urban growth left the station behind. Several years ago it was barely active, in a sorry state.

Then in 1989 Glendale purchased it to be a transportation center for Amtrak and Metrolink. The little survivor was placed on the National Register of Historic Places, and a new life began.

After a year of restoration, the depot is now fresh as a daisy and a joy to see even if you are not traveling anywhere. It would be fun to sketch, or to photograph. Two vine-laced pergolas lead to the entrance fountain. Creamy white finials against the (usually blue) sky seem to echo the minarets of Glendale's Brand Library. Tall palms add a tropical air.

The heavy wooden doors are replicas of the originals, framed with doorway swags of cream and gray plaster. The depot walls are reinforced concrete covered with lath and plaster to give the look of adobe. Their wavy smoothness looks like new. Decorative iron work is everywhere, in a great variety of designs.

Inside, the old beams are freshly stenciled in the original colors (surprise: these are concrete, not wood). Half the benches are original and half replicas; who could tell which are which?

Outside, the covered waiting area is trimmed with more stencils. Projects like this typically include some public art, so Los Angeles artist Lynn Goodpasture has created an outdoor clock with mosaic glass designs on each side: an artful way to see if the train, or the traveler, is on time.

How to get there: From the 134 Freeway, exit at Brand Blvd., drive south, turn right on San Fernando Rd. and left on Cerritos St. to the end.

Chinese Historical Society of Southern California
✧ *Los Angeles* ✧

IF YOU LIKE PONDERING the layers of history, you'll enjoy visiting the two little white houses on the northern edge of Chinatown in downtown Los Angeles.

These simple frame cottages are rare examples of working-class homes of the late 1880s, occupied by the Fritz family for more than a century. Today, they are home to the Chinese Historical Society of Southern California. What is their story?

Philipp Fritz was a native of Alsace who came to America in 1873. Like many other immigrants, he worked and saved to bring his wife and three sons to join him, which they did in 1884. Fritz was a carpenter for the Bridges and Buildings Department of the Southern Pacific Railroad, and there must have been work aplenty in those years of growth.

In 1886, Fritz bought two lots in the Bernard Tract, a multi-ethnic neighborhood once called Sonoratown. Here lived a mixture of Euro-

pean immigrants and native Californians of Mexican descent. Fritz built three small houses (one was moved away in the 1930s) in Queen Anne style, with decorated gables and simple porches. Inside are 12-foot ceilings and modestly ornamented woodwork and fixtures. Comfortable domestic spaces they were, and they became a family compound for Fritz relatives.

The granddaughter of Philipp Fritz, Louise Whiting, lived all of her 100 years in one or another of the cottages, until her death in 1992.

The houses have changed very little. Urbanization has surged nearby, but it has not swamped these two survivors. The biggest shift in their surroundings came with construction of Union Station railway depot in the 1930s. Old Chinatown east of Alameda Street was torn down, and a New Chinatown was established along Broadway and Hill Streets, just south of Bernard Street. Later the Pasadena Freeway (Arroyo Seco Parkway) was built right behind the Fritz houses, with Dodger Stadium just north of that.

After the death of the last Fritz, the cottages were bought by the Chinese Historical Society of Southern California in 1995. This Society was founded in 1975 to increase awareness of the Chinese-American heritage, which they actively do with programs, publications, tours, and undergraduate scholarships. Members are welcome to participate in trips and research projects.

In 1995, they were given some 200,000 artifacts excavated from Old Chinatown, Los Angeles, when the Metro Red Line was built beside Union Station. Some of these objects of daily life are displayed today in the Bernard Street cottages, while most are in storage.

Other exhibits show neighborhood life at that spot over the years. Yes, that is an oil derrick once in the backyard. Early maps indicate Consolidated Crude Oil Co. had its wells right behind the Bernard Street homes.

These are tiny houses, but they open up onto a wide history. You can buy a book or two, carefully researched, and then pick up a walking tour map of nearby Los Angeles Chinatown.

How to get there: 411 Bernard St. is between Broadway and Hill Sts., north of College St. Consult a local map or call (323) 222-0856.

175

Evergreen Memorial Park
✧ *Los Angeles* ✧

IT'S THE OLDEST, and so you know it has stories to tell. Founded in 1877, Evergreen Memorial Park is the oldest remaining cemetery in Los Angeles.

It began in controversy over whether a private company had the right to engage in the business of burials. At last the City Council agreed to this, and the land was set aside, east of the Los Angeles River, in the area now called Boyle Heights. Today in the cemetery each strand of our city's ethnic diversity can be traced back many years.

One of the early groups was the Russian-Armenians who came to Los Angeles soon after World War I. With them came the tradition of placing pictures on the grave stones. Even earlier were the Civil War veterans. The simple markers in their section sometimes just bear a name and a state, or a rank to indicate that they served with pride.

Pioneer families can be found, those who have left their names on streets and towns in the Southland. Members of the Hollenbeck and Workman families are here, also the Van Nuys family and the Lankershims. Jack Benny's faithful

176

"Rochester" (Eddie Anderson) is here, and others from radio and show business.

A striking memorial marks the area honoring American soldiers of Japanese ancestry who fought and died in World War II. The words of Generals Dwight Eisenhower and Mark Clark pay tribute to their bravery.

Farthest from the entrance, near the Lorena Street side of the cemetery, is a very old Chinese shrine (pictured here). Built in 1888, it is the oldest surviving structure of Chinese settlement in the Los Angeles area. In a little hollow are special markers and two ovens for the burning of paper money and incense, to send these provisions along with the deceased to the next world. This custom is still practiced, and the shrine is preserved by the Chinese Historical Society of Los Angeles (see the article about them in this book).

Special organizations have their sections to rest in peace together. One area was dedicated by circus and carnival troupes in 1922 for the Pacific Coast Showmen's Association. You'll find hints of their circus vocation in carvings on the grave stones.

A map of the sites and a brief history may be picked up as you enter Evergreen Memorial Park. Despite its name, the cemetery is not deeply shaded, but is quite open to a wide and bright sky. As you walk, you'll be impressed by the variety of memorial art favored through the ages, from Victorian mourning sculptures to more modern simplicity.

A Memorial Day Program is held here each year, and the public is welcome, to listen to music and honor the pioneers, the war dead, and the many others who are part of Los Angeles history.

How to get there: Evergreen Memorial Park is at 204 N. Evergreen Ave. From the 5 Freeway, exit at Cesar Chavez Ave. and drive east. Turn right on Evergreen Ave. to the entrance gates. Call (323) 268-6714 for information.

Southwest Museum
Ethnobotanical Garden
◇ *Highland Park* ◇

SOMETIMES what appears to be lost may only be hidden, and it may be found again by patiently seeking the old ways. Showing the original uses of California native plants is the mission of the Southwest Museum's Ethnobotanical Garden.

California has the largest native flora of any state. The abundant plant life served our original peoples for food, tools, clothing, shelter and medicine. Some of the common plants are now scarce, their habitats disappearing and their uses slipping from memory.

Several years ago curators at the Southwest Museum, one of the nation's most important Native American centers, decided that a living exhibit could remind us of this plant heritage.

The museum came from the collections and energy of Charles F. Lummis, librarian, journalist, and editor. He was a crusader for Native Americans, the California missions, and other Southwest causes. His museum was completed in 1914, a Mission Revival style building with a distinctive seven-story tower rising high above the Arroyo Seco. It's now a Los Angeles City Landmark.

The new garden (called "ethno-botanical," because it shows the practical uses of plants) is on a rounded hilltop below the museum. A committee of botanists, historians and Native Americans researched the plants. The California Conservation Corps cleared  terraced areas and planted in 1994 the sections for chaparral, riverbed, bog, desert, and medicine and dye plants. Now birds dip into a rush-edged pool, and you can feel the preciousness of water and shade on this sunny hillside.

In the chaparral section you'll find the elderberry tree. Its flat, pale yellow flower heads are familiar along the foothills. Local indigenous people made flutes, whistles and clappersticks from its wood, and they ate its leaves and berries (a good source of vitamin C). Tea made from its flowers could treat colds and fever. The twigs and leaves provided dyes, and the stems became arrow shafts.

No supermarkets? No hardware stores? Our predecessors in the Golden State found necessary resources growing right at hand. Other foods in this garden came from the coast live oak (acorns), manzanita, prickly pear, pinyon and jojoba. Dwellings were made from willow, tule and cattail. Baskets were woven from juncus and deer grass (up to 1000 stems needed to form a small basket). Medicines came from almost everything in the garden, and smoke of the white sage purified the spirit.

You can find California native plants around the Southland, but nowhere so close to the artifacts and photographs illustrating the old ways of life. In the museum, you'll see just the tip of their basket collection (which numbers about 11,000). Then step outside and see the fibers as they grow. Across the Arroyo, a view of grassy hills recalls open spaces.

This is a garden with stories to tell. The museum offers programs on Gabrielino/Tongva and Chumash uses of these beautiful and aromatic plants. In the words of the Native American elders: if the young will listen, the old will remember.

How to get there: The Southwest Museum is at 234 Museum Drive. From the 110 Freeway, exit at Avenue 43 and follow signs to the museum. Call (323) 221-2164.

Heritage Square Museum
✧ *Los Angeles* ✧

FREEWAY TRAVELERS heading downtown on the Pasadena Freeway pass an intriguing cluster of old buildings across the Arroyo Seco. They seem to have been left on the shore, somehow, as the stream of history rushed on.

This is Heritage Square Museum, a historic park preserving Victorian-era structures rescued from demolition and moved here. Seven buildings are in the collection, placed in a village setting.

The largest and smallest are survivors from Pasadena. The Lincoln Avenue Methodist Church (circa 1897) once stood on the corner of Orange Grove Boulevard and Lincoln Avenue (where the main post office is now). A solid 80 feet by 100 feet, the church has an elegant open-work tower and two monumental windows. Its exterior details include Carpenter Gothic, Queen Anne and Eastlake styles.

A little architectural echo is the Carriage Barn (1899) , a Gothic miniature once next to the Huntington Hospital in Pasadena. It has been used as the carpentry shop for restoration at the Square.

Pasadena's rare Octagon House (1893) is here too, awaiting work. It is one of the few examples of this form in California, rather an eccentric gem.

One of the earliest to reach the Square was the imposing Hale House (1887), with its ornate brick chimneys and stained glass windows. Its complex patterns of red and green paint are rather dazzling. The Mansard-style Valley Knudsen residence (1883) is small and snug. In front is a coral tree moved with the house and still doing well.

Note the hand-carved touches on the tiny Beaudry Street house (1887), once the home of John Ford, a wood carver. He covered the exterior with faces, sunbursts and trims. Only 20 by 30 feet in size, the little house prickles with personality.

The Palms Depot, over 100 years old, is one of the last wooden stations from the Southern Pacific Railroad. Fully restored, it wears an authentically-researched color now known to preservationists as Palms Depot Yellow.

Docents will take visitors into several of the buildings, and they comment on all the exteriors. Future ideas for the 10-acre site include a Victorian bandstand and a trolley linking the residential village to an area of vintage stores which may be added later.

This is no manicured "stage set." Heritage Square is clearly a work in progress. Inside the church, apprentice plasterers have donated work to practice their craft. Elsewhere, volun-

teers have shored up foundations and painted stairways. Piles of donated bricks and cobblestones wait to be made into a road.

Most of these buildings are just one step ahead of oblivion and need hours of restoration. But at least they are still with us, showing the imagination of an earlier time.

"Seeking comes before seeing," said art historian E.H. Gombrich. See for yourself the details and zest of this Victorian architecture. In the late 19th century land boom of Southern California, even the buildings had an air of optimism.

These illustrations show the Hale House (p. 180), the Valley Knudsen House (p. 181) and the Ford House (p. 182).

How to get there: Heritage Square Museum is at 3800 Homer St. From the 110 Freeway, exit at Avenue 43 and drive south, then right on Homer to its end. Call (626) 449-0193.

Sparkletts Water Company

✧ *Eagle Rock* ✧

OH, THOSE EXUBERANT 1920S, when architecture picked up just about any style, and the more the merrier. In Southern California from that decade you'll find buildings echoing English Tudor, Spanish Colonial, Mayan and Egyptian styles. Why not a Persian mosque?

In this mood of "period revival" architecture, Richard D. King designed in 1925 a desert oasis of a building, which still stands today as the Sparkletts Drinking Water Corporation in Eagle Rock.

The Eagle Rock valley was a fitting home for this palace of water. Under the watchful brow of its famous rock, the rural settlement was thriving by the turn of the twentieth century. Memoirs of early residents speak of apricot orchards, alfalfa, walnuts and plums, and especially the strawberry farms. Peanuts and beehives were there too, and "everyone in the valley kept a horse and a cow."

The community valued an artesian well, which flowed naturally all year. In 1923 Eagle Rock tried to secure the rights to this water

to avoid annexation to the city of Los Angeles, but they did not succeed.

In 1925, three partners—Glen Bollinger, Burton Arnds Sr. and Arthur Washburne—established the Sparkling Artesian Water Company to bottle the waters of the historic well. As publicity, they gave away free water for several weeks, since a broken aqueduct had turned the town's water muddy. Citizens gathered around with buckets and jars, and the business was launched.

The company soon changed its name to Sparkletts and adopted the bright green color for its delivery trucks. In 1928, the fledgling company sold over a million bottles of water, all from its own wells. The huge bottling plant, covering two city blocks in Eagle Rock, was completed in 1929.

The building is all of brick, painted white like a desert palace. The main entrance is under an arched opening, with a Persian-inspired ceramic tile mural above the entry. This tranquil work of art is well worth a closer look. There are smaller domes at the corners of the building, and a large roof-top sign with an old company logo.

Some of the original building is no longer there. After being damaged in the 1971 Sylmar earthquake, the entire north wing (once symmetrical with the south wing) was removed, as was a small tower and the minaret behind the main dome. But a small curving outside staircase remains, suggesting the possibility of a call to prayer.

The Sparkletts brand now belongs to the McKesson Water Products Company, and they still provide free water in times of disaster as they did in the 1920s. Architecture buffs love their classy building, well worth a detour if you are in the area. You'll see the details best and appreciate its rarity if you check it out on foot. Architectural historians David Gebhard and Robert Winter could not resist calling this "a mosque of the first water."

How to get there: The building is at 4500 York Blvd. From the 134 Freeway, exit at Colorado Blvd. and drive west. Turn left at Eagle Rock Blvd. and left on York.

Theodore Payne Foundation
and Nursery
✧ *Sun Valley* ✧

IN 1893, a young Englishman trotted down the beautiful Santiago Canyon in Orange County on his little mare named Kitty. He had just spent his 21st birthday at the World's Fair in Chicago, on his way from England to California. Ahead of him was the rambling white bungalow of his employer, the famed Polish actress, Madame Helena Modjeska.

He had been trained in the nursery business at home, and was now the gardener at this country estate. Soon he was enthralled with California's native plants and began his life's work, for this was Theodore Payne.

Young Payne next worked for Germain Seed Company, then set up his own nursery in Los Angeles in 1903. As he saw the California wildflowers disappearing from the landscape, he began to specialize in the native plants and their seeds.

To stir up interest, Payne offered to sow wildflower seeds in vacant lots around the Southland. Walter Raymond of South Pasadena's Raymond Hotel accepted, and his land sprouted a glorious spring display. Another of these "demonstration plots" was the corner of Lake Avenue and Colorado Boulevard in Pasadena, a vacant lot ablaze with colorful blooms (it's a major city intersection today).

Payne marked many accomplishments, including a five-acre wild garden in Exposition Park in Los Angeles and native gardens at Caltech (Pasadena) and Descanso Gardens (La Canada Flintridge). When he began his work, native plants were almost unknown in California nurseries. In his lifetime he brought over 430 species of them into the trade.

In 1961, ending 58 years in business, he helped establish the Theodore Payne Foundation, a non-profit organization to preserve California's flora. His long life brought him many honors, including a 90th birthday celebration in the chambers of the Los Angeles County Supervisors.

Today, Madame Modjeska's house, designed by the famed New York architect Stanford White in the 1880s, still stands in its oak-shaded canyon and can be visited (it's about 20 miles east of the city of Orange).

The legacy of the young man who tended her gardens is carried on in Sun Valley, a town beside the Verdugo Hills. Here the Theodore Payne nursery climbs the slopes of a 22-acre property. Old sycamores shade a picnic area. Wildflower Hill, a wild display garden with a trail winding upward, rises behind the rows of plants for sale.

The Foundation offers many programs to perpetuate the native flora: classes and workshops, the spring Wildflower Hotline, and a tempting bookstore. Neat cabinets store dozens of seed varieties, including mixtures formulated by Payne himself. You'll find Blue and Gold, Shady Mixture, Child's Garden, Butterfly Mixture, and many more. There is a sense of fellowship here, sharing all these riches straight from Mother Nature. The staff gives knowledgeable advice, then checks on your next visit: "How did your hummingbird sage do on that sunny slope?" These plants are content in Southern California, because they are at home.

How to get there: The Foundation is at 10459 Tuxford St. From the 210 Freeway, exit at La Tuna Canyon Rd. and drive west. Turn right on Wheatland Ave. and right on Tuxford. Call (818) 768-1802.

A Practical Index

These are casual groupings, just to suggest some combinations you might explore. Some sites appear more than once. Others defy categorizing and do not appear here at all. You may put together your own patterns and favorites.

Special Architecture

Special Gardens

Trees and Botanical Landmarks

Wide Open Spaces

...also the foothill lands around the Nature Centers

Women's Clubs

About the Author

Photo by Hortensia Chu

Elizabeth Pomeroy holds a Ph.D. in English from UCLA. She is an active Sierra Club member and teaches English at Pasadena City College. She has written articles on literature and history, and her recent books include *Reading the Portraits of Queen Elizabeth I* and *Lost and Found: Historic and Natural Landmarks of the San Gabriel Valley*, a selection from her regular newspaper columns on historic places. She is also the author of *John Muir: A Naturalist in Southern California*.

About the Artists

Joseph Stoddard is an artist who lives and works in Pasadena. He has produced many images for books, posters and magazines about the Southland and never goes anywhere without his sketch book and miniature paint box. A selection of his watercolors was recently published in the book *Pasadena Sketchbook*.

Hortensia Chu is a graphic designer and illustrator who also resides in Pasadena. She has designed many book covers and collaborated with Joseph Stoddard on other Southern California publications. She has been the art director for the projects of Many Moons Press.

Notes and Sketches

Notes and Sketches

Notes and Sketches